WHEN THE *Spirit* Says Sing!

A Brief History of African Slave Songs in the Americas

Truuke M. Ameigh

Cover Portrait by Susan L. Ameigh

NEWMAN SPRINGS PUBLISHING
320 Broad Street
Red Bank, NJ 07701

First originally published by Newman Springs Publishing 2024

ISBN 979-8-89061-111-6 (Paperback)
ISBN 979-8-89061-112-3 (Digital)

Printed in the United States of America

To the thousands who sing or have
sung these remarkable songs

C O N T E N T S

P R E F A C E

I first became acquainted with African American spirituals as a young person in my church, and my first memorable experience was in high school with the singing of "Soon Ah Will Be Done'" arranged by William T. Dawson. I delight in that arrangement to this day. I have directed and arranged spirituals for choirs and soloists ever since.

In 2009, I was teaching in an elementary school with a large African American population. My students enjoyed singing spirituals and the stories about the Underground Railroad that were associated with some of them. I decided to write a book for them. It was called *Gonna Sing!* and they enjoyed it immensely.

Later, I taught a course at a community college and began a more scholarly investigation. I became even more enamored of the subject. This manuscript is the product of that research.

When the Spirit Says Sing! A Brief History of African Slave Songs in the Americas is a description of differing forms of African spirituals as they developed in America. Among them are ring shouts, shanties, field hollers, jubilee songs, sorrow songs, work songs, and rhyming spirituals. This music found its way to Florida, the Bahamas, and Mexico, as well as the southern plantations with which they are usually associated, and evolved into styles that suited their cultures.

This book aims to share with the reader the story of spirituals as they took on the trappings of folksong and life associated with the Underground Railroad. It begins in Africa where the heritage of song and dance, so important to the spiritual, began.

I describe some of the early spirituals not necessarily associated with the Underground Railroad. I also include code songs and a discussion of spirituals up to the mid-twentieth century. For example, "Sometimes I Feel Like a Motherless Child" is a song about the feelings of an enslaved person in captivity. "Steal Away" is a code song that survives as a hymn in churches today with its original intent. "La Bamba" has African, Mexican, and Spanish roots but was a popular song in America in the 1950s. I have included information about Black Seminoles and their music as well.

Abolitionists, stationmasters, and conductors of the Underground Railroad such as William Still and William Lloyd Garrison are mentioned. I also include abolitionists and conductors such as Harriet Tubman and Frederick Douglass.

I have referred to artists who helped to make spirituals well-known. Among them are Marian Anderson, Harry T. Burleigh, and Kathleen Battle. Most of the songs are available on a computer or smart phone search. I suggest you use performances by African American artists in your searches as they are generally truer to the original intent of the spirituals.

A note concerning the suggested recordings: Some people may say that most of the arrangements selected are not authentic because, originally, spirituals were sung as a single line of music and a cappella. Slaves, for the most part, were not allowed instruments, and nearly all the spirituals I have chosen are arrangements with instrumental accompaniments. They are usually concert versions. I believe that the songs are so strong rhythmically and melodically that the intended spirit doesn't get lost in translation. Those who want to hear them as originally sung need to access a research library such as the Library of Congress. Few examples are available, even in that kind of search.

The lyrics printed in this book do not always match the spiritual suggested for listening. For the most part, the lyrics I have selected are more representative of renditions by enslaved peoples. Dialect is used, but not consistently. There are always numerous versions of lyrics in most spirituals, and those in this book are selected for their accessibility.

It has been marvelous to listen to and learn about these wonderful songs. It has been amazing as a professor, teacher, choir director, and composer to know exactly how impactful these songs are. They are songs that will never die. The history surrounding them is a testament to the invincible character of the slave in a world that opposed him at every turn. Today, as "Black Lives Matter" and other such groups raise the consciousness of the general population, this study should lift African American spirituals to new heights and bring recognition of a rich heritage to people everywhere.

African Origins and the Ring Shout

There is a genre of song in America referred to as the African American spiritual. African citizens created it. People were shipped to America as early as the sixteenth century, not as settlers but as enslaved persons. Traditionally, the first enslaved people in America came ashore in 1619 at the colony of Jamestown, Virginia. There were twenty of them. The first slaves actually arrived in Florida in 1539. Since Florida belonged to Spain at that time and was not associated with the slavery familiar to the rest of the continent, that fact is not often mentioned.

In Africa, tribes frequently fought one another and sometimes captured other Africans, keeping them as slaves. Some say that the enslaved were well treated by the African community.[1] Others say that enslaved persons in Africa were treated more cruelly than in America.[2] Whether either is true, we do know that Africans were familiar with slavery long before enslaved persons reached American shores. In this text, however, we will explore the music of Africa as it pertains to the road to freedom in the Americas.

The journey to America was horrendous for enslaved persons, who generally spent their trip in the bowels of a ship. The conditions were extremely crowded and unsanitary. Quarters were often so cramped that they could not stretch, much less stand or walk. The people were usually kept in irons. If any person was perceived as ill or weak, he was thrown overboard. Their only belongings were, literally, the shirts on their backs. When they reached America, they were sold to the highest bidder with no thought as to family connections or concern for personal welfare.

The enslaved were imported mostly from Western and Central Africa. Few of them spoke the same language, and they certainly did not speak English or Spanish. Those who spoke the same language were separated to prevent revolt. Ultimately, the ability to verbally communicate was lost, so they turned to song and dance for communication. It was the perfect choice because the roles of music and dance in the countries of Western and of Central Africa were amazingly similar and essential features of daily life. Remnants of this kind of song continued well into the twentieth century.

An example of a song and dance that lasted for days in Africa is the ring shout. A ring shout is a dance with a song, performed in a counterclockwise circle either by a group or by an individual. Visitors to Africa recognize a strong resemblance between indigenous African dance and this American cousin. The content of the songs that evolved from the African ring shout eventually came to include material drawn from the Bibles of the singers' captors, and especially from stories of the Old Testament. When people talk about spirituals, they are usually referring to songs created in slavery, containing themes from Jewish and Christian traditions. It is probable that the following ring shout, "Oh, Eve, Where Is Adam," is an African song and dance with American lyrics.

Oh, Eve, Where Is Adam

Oh, Eve where is Adam?
Oh, Eve where is Adam?
Oh, Eve where is Adam?
Adam in the garden Pinnin' leaves.
Adam in the garden Pinnin' leaves.

Lord called Adam,
Lord called Adam,
Lord called Adam,

Adam in the garden pinnin' leaves.
Adam in the garden pinnin' leaves.

Adam wouldn' answer Pinnin' leaves.

Adam shame' Pinnin' leaves.

Adam (rising inflection) Pinnin' leaves.

Adam (falling inflection) Pinnin' leaves.

Where't thou? Pinnin' leaves.

Adam naked. Pinnin' leaves.

Ain't y'u shame'? Pinnin' leaves.

Lord I'm shame'. Pinnin' leaves.

(Available online. Suggested performer: McIntosh Country Shouters)

A good description of the ring shout is found in the book *Bahama Songs and Stories* by Charles L. Edwards.

When the "Sperichil" is struck up, they begin their first walking, and by and by, shuffling around, one after the other in a ring. The foot is hardly taken from the floor, and the progression is mainly due to a jerking, hitching motion, which agitates the entire shouter, and soon brings out streams of perspiration. Sometimes they dance silently, sometimes as they shuffle, they sing the chorus of the spiritual, and sometimes the song itself is also sung by the dancers. But more frequently a band, composed of some of the best singers and of tired shouters, stand at the side of the room to "base" the others, singing the body of the song and clapping their hands together or on their knees.[3]

Spirituals evolved as a union between African rhythm and melody and American lyrics and religion. "Oh, Eve, Where Is Adam" is sung in question-and-answer style (a gift from Africa often used in spirituals). It is a Bible story, popular in slave songs. However, Bible stories were not sung when the earliest enslaved people arrived. Africans practiced their own religions for quite a while before Christianity became popular among them.

There are many different variations of the following ring shout called "Plumb de Line." The terms *deacon*, *sister*, and *brother* are sometimes substituted for the term *member* in this spiritual. The term *deacon* refers to the person who lined out the song. In other words, he would sing or deacon the lines, and the group would repeat them. It is the same kind of singing that was done early in seventeenth-century churches.[4] It allowed the illiterate to sing songs that they were unable to read. In slavery, where illiteracy was the norm, it allowed slave leaders, or deacons, to teach songs they already knew or which they composed themselves. This spiritual is a call-and-response song.

Plumb de Line

Member,
Plumb de line.
Member,
Plumb de line.
Member,
Plumb de line.
Want t' go t' heaven got a plumb de line.

You got t' sing right
Plumb de line.
You got t' sing right
Plumb de line.

You got t' sing right
Plumb de line.
Want t' go t' heaven got a plumb de line.

O sister,
Plumb de line.
O sister,
Plumb de line.
O sister,
Plumb de line.
Want t' go t' heaven got a plumb de line.

You got t' shout right
Plumb de line.
You got t' shout right
Plumb de line.
You got t' shout right
Plumb de line.
Want t' go t' heaven got a plumb de line.

(Available online. Suggested performer: Bessie Jones)

"Plumb the line" refers to a builder's tool, the plumb line, that helps a builder create exact vertical measurements for his work. Today's equivalent is the level. If one is going to "plumb de line," he is going to be an upstanding individual.

"Plumb de Line" and "Pharaoh's Hos' Got Lost" are ring shouts that hearken from South Carolina. "Pharaoh's Hos' Got Lost" was also performed as a tradition by Georgia Sea Island descendants in the community of Bolden, Georgia.

African Americans set the music with the beating of a broom handle on the wooden floor. They call the stepping and beating of the broom "the shout," and they distinguish between shouters (those who step and move in the ring) and the singer (leader), basers (other singers), and stickers (broom beaters).[5] Like most ring shouts "Pharaoh's Hos' Got Los'" has a religious theme. There is irregular clapping by the group to illustrate the chaos of the host of soldiers getting lost. In the following transcription, L = leader, L and B = leader and basers, and Ch = all present.

Pharaoh's Hos' Got Los

L: *Moses, Moses lay your rod*
L&B: *In that Red Sea*
L: *Lay your rod, let the children crossing*
L&B: *In that Red Sea.*
Ch: *Ol' Pharaoh's hos' got los', los', los',*
Ol' Pharaoh's hos' got los' In that Red Sea.
They shout when the hos' got los', los', los',
They shout when the hos' got los',
In that Red Sea.

L: *Moses, Moses, lay your rod*
L&B: *In that Red Sea*
L: *Lay your rod, let the children cross*
L&B: *In that Red Sea.*
Ch: *Ol' Pharaoh's hos' got los', los', los'*
Pharaoh's hos' got los',
In that Red Sea.

L: *Oh Moses, please lay your rod*
L&B: *In that Red Sea*
L: *Lay your rod, let the children cross*
L&B: *In that Red Sea.*
Ch: *Ol' Pharaoh's hos' got los', los', los'*
Pharaoh's hos' got los', los', los'
Such a weepin' when the hos' got los'
In that Red Sea.

(Available online. Suggested performer: the McIntosh Country Shouters)

A definite timeline for use of spirituals in the United States is murky because it was an oral tradition. Enslaved persons were generally unable to read and write language, much less read and write music. In most cases, their owners would not permit education, so it fell to slaves to pass on their songs by rote. African music would have been difficult to write in any case as it used polyrhythms, sophisticated syncopation, scales that included tones to which Americans were unaccustomed, and sounds unfamiliar to those educated in the European tradition. An example of unfamiliar sounds are the rising and falling inflection of "Adam" in the fifth and sixth verse of "Oh, Eve, Where Is Adam." It gives the impression of the voice of God calling for Adam.

The American South, where most enslaved people resided, was not eager to recognize cultural achievement in its African population. Despite approximately a century and a half of singing spirituals, it wasn't until a tour by the Fisk University Jubilee Singers in 1872 that spirituals gained any serious recognition from the musical community at large.

Song and dance brought from Africa proved to be a huge resource in the creation of the African American spiritual. When coupled with the Bible and creativity of enslaved people, the results were a testimony to their endurance under horrific circumstances and an ode to their indomitable spirit.

---

[1] James Lovell Jr., *Black Song: The Forge and the Flame* (New York: The Macmillan Company, 1972), p. 35.

[2] Lydia Parrish, *Slave Songs of the Georgia Sea Islands* (Athens: The University of Georgia Press, 1992), p. 24.

[3] Charles C. Edwards, *Bahamas Songs and Spirituals* (London: Forgotten Books, 2015), p. 108.

[4] Lydia Parrish, *Slave Songs of the Georgia Sea Islands* (Athens: University of Georgia Press, 1992), p. 68.

[5] Art Rosenbaum, Margo Newmark Rosenbaum, and Johann S. Buis, *Shout Because You're Free* (Athens and London: University of Georgia Press, 2013), p. 2.

CHAPTER 2

Sorrow Songs

"Many spirituals, known as 'sorrow songs,' are intense, slow[,] and melancholic"[1] and reflect the struggles of slavery. The label was given to them by African American historian W. E. B. Du Bois. "Sometimes I Feel Like a Motherless Child" is such. It is not a "story song"; it is a cry of the anguish experienced by every person touched by the plight of a child on the auction block. African culture was communal in nature, which is why so many spirituals refer to brother and sister (not necessarily biological siblings), but unlike them, this song refers to the mother-child connection and makes the song an even more poignant lament.

As with the song "Oh, Eve, Where Is Adam," the first three lines are repeated followed by the last two lines. The last verse, "true believer," is only sung twice rather than three times as in the other verses. It is sung as a wail, perhaps to make a sarcastic point about the Christian behavior of the person who put the child there. The African slave was not above including sarcasm in the lyrics of his songs.

Sometimes I Feel Like a Motherless Child

Sometimes I feel like a motherless child,
Sometimes I feel like a motherless child,
Sometimes I feel like a motherless child,

A long way from home
A long way from home

Sometimes I feel like I'm almost done,
Sometimes I feel like I'm almost done,
Sometimes I feel like I'm almost done,

A long way from home, A long way from home.
True believer, True believer,
A long way from home, A long way from home.

(Available online. Suggested performer: Odetta)

Sometimes crying is the only thing that will help. There is another sorrow song called "Wring My Hands and Cry" that sums it all up.

Wring My Hands and Cry

Sometimes I feel like a moanin' dove,
Sometimes I feel like a moanin' dove,
Wring my han's an' cry, cry, cry
Wring my han's an' cry, cry.

(Available online. Suggested performance: Robert Shaw Chorale)

Just knowing he was caught in an oppressive world sometimes caused a slave to feel he was constantly running for his life, as described in the following sorrow spiritual, "Runnin' fo' My Life."

Runnin' fo' My Life

Ef ennybody ax yo' what's de matter wid me,
Ef ennybody ax yo' what's de matter wid me,
Jis tell him I say I'm runnin' fo' my life.
Jis tell him I say I'm runnin' fo' my life.

Ef ennybody ax yo' what's de matter wid me,
Ef rnnybody ax yo' what's de matter wid me,
Jis tell him I'm mo'nin' fo' my life.
Js tell him I'm mo'nin' fo' my life.

Ef ennybody ax yo' what's de matter wid me,
Ef ennybody ax yo' what's de matter wid me,
Jis tell him I'm prayin' fo' my life.
Jis tell him I'm prayin' fo' my life.

(Available online. Suggested performer: Rev. Timothy Wright)

Many are and have been amazed at the ability of the enslaved to triumph over the degradation of their experience. They usually had little food, and what they had was of poor quality. They sometimes got one or two sets of clothing per year, and they worked long and hard, often from sunrise to sunset and even beyond. Many experienced whippings at the least little whim of the master or overseer. Music brought them solace and, to some extent, even hope.[2] "The songs of the slave represent the sorrows, rather than the joys, of his heart; he is relieved by them only as an aching heart is relieved by its tears."[3]

The languages of slave owners were different. French, English, German, and Spanish owners were common. Since education was not a high priority for slaves nor even for slaveowners, for that matter, dialect developed. There were many local dialects at the time, but because of televisions in every home and a cell phone in every pocket, the use of the nineteenth-century dialect in spirituals has pretty much gone by the wayside.

Some slaveowners lived on small farms where the whole family worked the fields. There was little, if any, time for school. Few of the enslaved were as lucky as Frederick Douglass during his young life, who lived in a sophisticated household where he learned his alphabet and early reading skills from his mistress. Dialect in songs persisted whole or in part. Such is the case in the following spiritual. "Nobody

Knows de Trouble I Seen" is a call-and-response song with a leader (L) singing the beginning measures and a group (G) responding.

Nobody Knows de Trouble I Seen

L: *Nobody knows de trouble I seen,*
Nobody knows but Jesus,
Nobody knows de trouble I seen,
G: *Glory Hallelujah.*

L: *Nobody knows de trouble I seen,*
Nobody knows my sorrow,
Nobody knows de trouble I seen,
G: *Glory Hallelujah.*

L: *Sometimes I'm up,*
Sometimes I'm down,
G: *Oh yes Lord.*
L: *Sometimes I'm almost to de ground.*
G: *Oh yes Lord.*

L: *Nobody knows de trouble I seen,*
Nobody knows but Jesus,
Nobody knows de trouble I seen,
G: *Glory Hallelujah.*

(Available online. Suggested performer: Louis Armstrong)

There is no dialect used in the following sorrow song, "I'm Troubled in Mind," though it surely contained it originally. For instance, *help* would be *hep*, *to* would be *t*, and *for* would be *fo*. Dialect, or lack thereof, depended on who transcribed the spiritual and where in the country the slave resided. Probably sung by freed slaves late in the nineteenth century (or it could be that verses were added at that time), it is both a lament and a statement of faith. As with most spirituals, there are different versions.

I'm Troubled in Mind

I'm troubled, I'm troubled
I'm troubled in mind.
If Jesus don't help me
I surely will die.

Oh, Jesus my savior,
On Thee I'll depend,
When troubles are near me
You'll be my true friend.

I'm troubled, I'm troubled,
I'm troubled in mind.
If Jesus don't help me
I surely will die.

When ladened with troubles
And burdened with grief.
To Jesus in secret
I'll go for relief.

In dark days of bondage
To Jesus I prayed
To help me to bear it,
And He gave me His aid.

I'm troubled, I'm troubled,
I'm troubled in mind.

If Jesus don't help me
I surely will die.

(Available online. Suggested performer: Barbara Hendricks)

"I'm Troubled in Mind" allowed the singer to express his or her feelings in a transformative way. Much like other people who have survived trauma, the enslaved person could access feelings about slavery and perhaps find the solace their circumstances required in song. Today, when a therapist asks a patient to talk about their feelings after a traumatic event in their life, by talking it through, the patient finds relief in a similar fashion.[4]

"Lord, How Come Me Here" is certainly a sorrow song. It describes graphically the feelings of a slave in bondage.

Lord, How Come Me Here

Lord, how come me here?
Lord, how come me here?
Lord, how come me here?
I wish I never was born.

There ain't no freedom here, Lord
There ain't no freedom here,
There ain't no freedom here,
I wish I never been born.

Lord, how come me here…

They treat me so mean here, Lord
They treat me so mean here,
They treat me so mean here,
I wish I never been born.

Lord, how come me here…

There's so much in the way, Lord
There's so much in the way,
There's so much in the way,
I wish…

Lord, how come me here…

(Available online. Suggested performer: Kathleen Battle)

Not a "sorrow song" but an example of how strong the desire for freedom persisted in the minds of some Africans is the following story:

> A cargo of slaves of the Ebo tribe had been landed at a suspiciously secluded spot on the west side of the island [in Georgia]. They preferred death to a life in captivity, and as they walked into the water the leader said: "The water brought us here. The water will take us away."[5]

The song associated with this mass suicide was "Oh, Freedom!"

Oh, Freedom!

Oh freedom, Oh freedom,
Oh, freedom over me,
And before I'd be a slave
I'd be buried in my grave,
And go home to my Lord and be free.

No more weepin', no more weepin'
No more weepin' over me

And before I'd be a slave
I'd be buried in my grave,
And go home to my Lord and be freed.

(Available online. Suggested performer: Harry Belafonte)

Spirituals often delve into the depths of despair. The spirituals mentioned in this chapter speak to the sorrows of the enslaved's lives and give poignant examples of the agony of their being. "Nobody Knows de Trouble I Seen" uses dialect, although when first sung, it probably used more. Research references that date from the nineteenth and early twentieth centuries depend much more heavily on dialect than those of the present day. With or without dialect, spirituals remain an enormous contribution to the history of folksong in America.

---

[1] "African American Spirituals," Library of Congress.
[2] Frederick Douglass, *My Bondage and My Freedom* (Odin's Library Classics), p. 134.
[3] Frederick Douglass, *My Bondage and My Freedom*, p. 34.
[4] Arthur C. Jones, *Wade in the Water* (Boulder: Leave A Little Room, 2005), p. 34.
[5] Lydia Parrish, *Slave Songs of the Georgia Sea Islands* (Athens, Georgia: University of Georgia Press, 1969), p. 37.

Jubilee Songs

Because slaves rarely were allowed instruments to accompany group singing, hand clapping was the norm, as was foot stomping. Believe it or not, owners were afraid for enslaved people to have drums as they (the owners) were always afraid of mutiny. You may wonder why drums might cause a mutiny.

Drum communication was common in Africa.[1] In fact, some version of drum playing there is referred to as "talking drums." It is said that "talking drums" were used to communicate among the enslaved to start a revolt in Stono, South Carolina. Twenty-five colonists and thirty-five to fifty African Americans were killed. (Some sources claim quite a few more.) Thereafter, there was a law prohibiting drums among African Americans in South Carolina. Other southern states followed suit. They didn't want another rebellion of such magnitude to happen again on American soil.

After drums were banned, enslaved people created rhythmic music by slapping their knees, thighs, arms, and other body parts in what was called "pattin' juba." It dates from the latter half of the eighteenth century.

In the Stono Rebellion, as it came to be called, slaves were attempting to escape south to Florida (which was in closer proximity to South Carolina and Georgia). In fact, slavery was introduced to Florida as early as 1539 when Hernando De Soto attempted to create a settlement there. At that time, many slaves would disappear into the wilderness to build a life of freedom. When Florida became a state in 1845, it joined as a slave state, and the enslaved continued to escape into the wilderness. There they were free to build their own lives away from slave owners and bounty hunters.

Jubilees or camp meetings, gatherings much like today's religious revivals, were highly charged emotional events that provided social and spiritual support to all who attended. They became popular with African Americans toward the end of slavery when Christianity became more attractive to the slave population.

"Rock o' My Soul" is a traditional African American spiritual that is sometimes referred to as a jubilee song or camp meeting song.[2] It is a spiritual that allows for pattin' juba. It is fast, rhythmic, and often syncopated: a rollicking tune, with plenty of room for hand clapping or other types of percussive sound.

Rock o' My Soul

Rock o' my soul in de bosom of Abraham,
Rock o' my soul in de bosom of Abraham,
Rock o' my soul in de bosom of Abraham.
Lord, rock o' my soul, King Jesus

So high, can't get over it
So low can't get under it
So wide can't get round it,
Lord, rock o' my soul.

Rock o' my soul in de bosom of Abraham,
Rock o' my soul in de bosom of Abraham,
Rock o' my soul in de bosom of Abraham,
Lord, rock o' my soul.

(Available online. Suggested performer: Louis Armstrong)

Another jubilee song is "In That Great Gettin' Up Mornin'." Sometimes referred to as "Fare Thee Well," it is also reliant on hand clapping and other percussive sounds. It dates from the nineteenth century and is a call-and-response spiritual, with the leader singing the lyrics while improvising and the group responding with "Fare thee well, fare thee well." The group might also improvise, but usually, they just answer.

In That Great Gettin' up Mornin'

In that great gettin' up mornin'
Fare thee well, fare thee well.
In that great gettin' up mornin'
Fare thee well, fare thee well.

I'm a-gonna tell you 'bout the comin' of the Savior.
Fare thee well, fare thee well.
I'm a-gonna tell you 'bout the comin' of the Savior.
Fare thee well, fare thee well.
I'm a-gonna tell you 'bout the comin' of the Savior
Fare thee well, fare thee well.

There's a better day a-comin'.
Fare thee well, fare thee well.
There's a better day a-comin'
Fare Thee well, fare thee well
There's a better day a-comin',
Fare thee well fare thee well.

Oh, preacher fold your Bible.
Fare thee well, fare thee well.
Oh, preacher fold your Bible,
Fare thee well, fare thee well
Oh, preacher fold your Bible
Fare thee well, fare thee well.

In that great gettin' up mornin'
Fare thee well, fare Thee well,
In that great getting' up mornin'
Fare thee well, fare thee well.
In that great getting' up mornin'
Fare thee well, fare thee well.

Gabriel, blow your trumpet.
Fare thee well, fare thee well,
Lord, how loud shall I blow it?
Fare thee well, fare thee well,
Loud as seven peals of thunder.
Fare thee well, fare thee well,
Wake the livin' nations
Fare thee well, fare thee well.

In that great gettin' up mornin'
Fare thee well, fare thee well,
In that great getting' up mornin'
Fare thee well, fare thee well,
Fare thee well, fare thee well

(Available online. Suggested performer: Mahalia Jackson)

"Ain't That Good News" is a jubilee song from the end of the Civil War. Probably a camp meeting song, it is lively and happy. It tells not of the Underground Railroad but of heaven.

Ain't That Good News

I've got a crown up in that kingdom,
Ain't that good news!
I've got a crown up in that kingdom,
Ain't that good news!

I'm a gonna lay down this world,
Gonna shoulder up my cross.
Gonna take it home to Jesus,
Ain't that good news!

I've got a harp up in that kingdom…
I'm a gonna lay down this world…
I've got a robe up in that kingdom…
I'm a gonna lay down this world…

(Available online. Suggested performer: Choral Project)

At this time, in the history of spirituals, the lyrics often referred to freedom from bondage as well as the more obvious meaning of the song. The issue of the final judgment of God, either on judgment day or in the promised land on earth, was one of these underlying messages, always lurking beneath such songs.[3]

Another spiritual, which was probably sung at camp meetings, is "This Little Light of Mine."

> The idea comes from John, a book in the Bible. "Let your light so shine before men, that they might see your good works, and glorify your Father which is in heaven."[4] The slave developed his own special slant, with little or no theology in it. Though it is just a little light, any bit of light can penetrate a mighty lot of darkness.[5]

This Little Light of Mine

This little light of mine, I'm goin' t' let it shine,
This little light of mine, I'm goin' t' let it shine,
This little light of mine, I'm goin' t' let it shine,
Let it shine, let it shine, let it shine.

All through the night, I'm goin' t' let it shine,
All through the night, I'm goin' t' let it shine,
All through the night, I'm goin' t' let it shine,
Let it shine, let it shine, let it shine.

Everywhere I go, I'm goin' t' let it shine,
Everywhere I go, I'm goin' t' let it shine
Everywhere I go, I'm goin' t' let it shine,
Let it shine, let it shine, let it shine.

This little light of mine, I'm goin' t' let it shine,
This little light of mine, I'm goin' t' let it shine,
This little light of mine, I'm goin' t' let it shine,
Let it shine, let it shine, let it shine.

(Available online. Suggested performer: Odetta)

Jubilee songs were sung by groups and were fast and rhythmic, including syncopation and improvisation. Performance often entailed the use of hand clapping and other forms of percussive sound. If it was call and response or question and answer, the leader improvised. Often the group improvised as well. "Little David Play on Your Harp" is a call-and-response spiritual.

Little David Play on Your Harp

Little David, play on your harp, hallelu, hallelu,
Little David, play on your harp, hallelu!
Little David, play on your harp, hallelu, hallelu,
Little David, play on your harp, hallelu!

Little David was a shepherd boy,
He killed Goliath and shouted for joy!

Little David, play on your harp, hallelu, hallelu,
Little David, play on your harp, hallelu!

Little David, ply on your harp, hallelu, hallelu,
Little David, play on your harp, hallelu!

Joshua was the son of Nun,
He never would quit 'til the work was done.

Little David, play on your harp…

(Available online. Suggested performer: Mahalia Jackson)

"Climbin' Up the Mountain Children!" combines both the theme of Judgment Day and the quick percussion and rhythm of a jubilee song.

Climbin' Up the Mountain Children!

Good Lord, I'm climbin' up the mountain children,
Ain't got long here to stay
If I nevermore see you again,
I'll meet you at the Judgement Day.

Daniel in the lion's den,
He began to pray,
The angel of the Lord locked the lion's jaw,
And Daniel went his way.
Good Lord, I'm climbin' up the mountain…

Hebrew children in the fire
They began to pray,
The angel of the Lord put the fire out,
And the children went their way.

Good Lord, I'm climbin' up the mountain…
Ain't got long here to stay

If I nevermore see you again,
I'll meet you at the Judgement Day.

(Available online. Suggested performer: Kaoma)

Most of these jubilee songs came about toward the end of slavery. Judgment Day was a popular theme then. Slaves always yearned for freedom from bondage, and it represented that. As all spirituals proved, their creators were poets. "This Little Light of Mine" is especially poetic as it transforms biblical scripture into a philosophy that even a child can appreciate.

---

[1] Francis Bebey, *African Music A People's Art*, translated by Josephine Bennett (Chicago, Lawrence Hill Books, 1975), p. 14.
[2] "African American Spirituals," Library of Congress.
[3] William Francis Allen, Slave Songs of the United States.
[4] Matthew 5:16 KJV.
[5] John Lovell Jr., *Black Song, The Forge and the Flame* (New York, The Macmillan Company, 1975), p. 288.

Work Songs, Field Hollers, and Shanties

Another kind of spiritual to consider is the work song, a group song with a leader. Singing usually accompanied work in Africa because so much work was of a rhythmic nature. It also set a tempo for work, which made it more efficient when slaves were working in groups. It continued the same in America.

Because music in Africa could not be divorced from religion, the tradition continued in America, and there are often biblical references found in these songs. For rowing on a river or bay, which is certainly a rhythmic task, the rowers might sing "Michael Row the Boat Ashore."[1] Note that the song mentions the Jordan River, hallelujah, jubilee, and Michael (an angel in Christian tradition), all references to religion.

Michael Row the Boat Ashore

Michael row the boat ashore, Hallelujah,
Michael row the boat ashore, Hallelujah.
Sister help to trim the sails, Hallelujah,
Sister help to trim the sails, Hallelujah.

Jordan's river is deep and wide, Hallelujah,
And I've got a home on the other side.

Michael row the boat ashore, Hallelujah,
Michael row the boat ashore, Hallelujah.

Michael's boat is a music boat, Hallelujah,
Michael's boat is a music boat, Hallelujah.
Michael row the boat ashore, Hallelujah,
Michael row the boat ashore, Hallelujah.

Trumpets sound the jubilee, Hallelujah,
Trumpets sound for you and me, Hallelujah.
Michael row the boat ashore, Hallelujah,
Michael row the boat ashore, Hallelujah.

(Available online. Suggested performer: Harry Belafonte)

The cotton gin invented by Eli Whitney in 1793 was a true revolution in the world of slavery. "Before that time, cotton fibers had to be separated from seeds by hand. To clean a pound of cotton took a full day. It was a long and tedious job…cotton was expensive."[2]

With the advent of the cotton gin, farmers who had grown tobacco, rice, and indigo began to cultivate cotton. The price of prime cotton lands tripled, and slavery moved west. Cotton production skyrocketed.[3] Therefore, the need for slave labor skyrocketed too. The next spiritual, a work song, hailed from those days. "Jump Down, Turn Around, Pick a Bale of Cotton" is boisterous, also rhythmic in nature, but it did not refer to the Bible.

Jump Down, Turn Around, Pick a Bale of Cotton

Jump down, turn around to pick a bale of cotton,
Jump down, turn around to pick a bale a day.
Jump down, turn around to pick a bale of cotton,
Jump down, turn around to pick a bale a day.

Oh, Lordy, pick a bale of cotton,
Oh Lordy, pick a bale a day.
Oh, Lordy, pick a bale of cotton,
Oh, Lordy, pick a bale a day.

Me and my buddy can pick a bale of cotton,
Me and my buddy can pick a bale a day.
Me and my buddy can pick a bale of cotton,
Me and my buddy can pick a bale a day.

Oh, Lordy, pick a bale of cotton,
Oh, Lordy, pick a bale a day.
Oh, Lordy, pick a bale of cotton,
Oh, Lordy, pick a bale a day.

Me and old Bill...

Oh, Lordy...

Jump, down...

Me and my wife...

Oh, Lordy...

Jump, down...

Me and my papa...

Oh, Lordy...

Jump, down...

(Available online. Suggested performer: Lonnie Donegan)

Work songs were often religious songs that adapted well to the task at hand. Such is the case with "Bye and Bye I'm Goin' t' See the King." This story probably dates from the early twentieth century.

> It was over the washboard that many a singer gave free scope to a religious turn of mind. "Bye and Bye I'm Goin' t' See the King" was once heard sung by a passerby. When asked where it came from, the washerwoman, who was doing the singing, replied that she had made it up. He thereupon reported to the newspapers that new spirituals were born every day.[4]

It turns out it was a very old song, but the story demonstrates how religion, work, and song were intertwined in the days of slavery.

By an' By-e I'm Goin' t' See the King

By an' by-e I'm goin' t' see the King.
By an' by-e I'm goin' t' see the King.
By an' by-e I'm goin' t' see the King.
Lord, I wouldin' mind dyin' if dyin' was all.

Wouldn' mind dyin' but I got t' go by myself.
Wouldn' mind dyin' but I got t' go by myself.
Wouldn' mind dyin' but I got t' go by myself,
Lord, I wouldn' mind dyin' if dyin' was all.

(Available online. Suggested performer: Blind Willie Johnson)

As stated earlier, spirituals were an oral tradition; therefore, there are many variations on the verses and different numbers of verses as well. Here is a different variation on "Bye and Bye I'm Goin' t' See the King."

> *Wouldn' mind dyin' but I got t' lay in the grave so long,*
> *Wouldn' mind dyin' but I got t' lay in the grave so long,*
> *Wouldn' mind dyin' but I got t' lay in the garve so long,*
> *Lord, I wouldn' mind dyin' if dyin' was all.*

Field hollers might be called work songs, the main difference being that a field holler was sung by an individual. Another difference was that the field holler had a flexible rhythm, and the work song had a steady beat. Falsetto, sudden changes of pitch, and portamento (gliding from one pitch to another) were occasionally employed in field hollers. They often began with moaning or humming and broke into song now and then, with a response coming from another slave in a different field far away.[5] Since moaning and groaning are a large part of a field holler, they are difficult to transcribe. One such is "Arwhoolie," which is a cornfield holler.

(Available online. Suggested performer: American Folk Music [Southern]: Cornfield Holler)

Shanties are another kind of work song. They usually reference sailing. When a plantation is near a navigable river or salt water, songs like "Stevedore's in Trouble, Carry 'im to the Aly-mo" (a stevedore is a member of a ship's crew) and "Sandy Anna" may be heard. Both carry in their titles the date of their inception and obviously hark back to the period of the Mexican War. Although they did not necessarily mention water, they were sung by sailors.

Shanties mention Australia and Rio along with "Go 'round the Horn, Yalla Gal, Go 'round the Horn" and suggest the period of the windjammer.[6] Australia was an option for escaped slaves and free African Americans who managed to sign on board a ship as sailors. They could sail on to San Francisco from there. Rio probably referred to the Rio Grande, the river border between Texas and Mexico. "Go 'round the Horn" suggested that escape could be realized by sailing around Cape Horn and north, again, to San Francisco. The following shanty, "Haul Away, I'm a Rollin' King," refers to Australia.

Haul Away, I'm a Rollin' King

Haul away, I'm a rollin' king.
Haul away, haul away
I'm boun' for South Australia.
Yonder come a flounder flat on the groun'
Haul away, haul away
I'm boun' for South Australia.
Belly to the groun' an' back to the sun
Haul away, haul away
I'm boun' for South Australia.

(Available online. Suggested performer: The Pogues)

There is a huge variety in types of work songs. There are songs used for rowing in a river, and others used for housework. Some were used for picking cotton. Hollers were used for a variety of crops. Shanties were used with navigable rivers and at sea.

Work songs, which set a tempo for a task, are usually rhythmic in nature and often religious or have references to religion. Shanties are the exception. Although rhythmic, they are not religious. There are hundreds of work songs, seemingly enough for every kind of task that requires hard labor.

---

[1] John Lovell Jr., *Black Song: the Forge and the Fire* (New York, The Macmillan Company, 1972), p. 194.
[2] Alice L. Baumgartner, *South to Freedom* (New York: Basic Books, 2020), p. 14.
[3] Alice L. Baumgartner, *South to Freedom*, p. 14.
[4] Lydia Parrish, *Slave Songs of the Georgia Sea Islands* (Athens, Georgia: University Press, 1969), p. 4.
[5] Michel Martin, In Song: Sounds of Slavery Listen to a holler (NPR).
[6] Lydia Parrish, *Slave Songs of the Georgia Sea Islands*, p. 15.

C H A P T E R   5

———

Spirituals Referencing Jesus's Life

Spirituals referencing the life of Christ date mostly from the Civil War era. Few are known for celebrating the birth of Jesus before that; what freemeh celebrated as a religious holiday for slaves was one given over to whiskey and coming and going at will. It was a way to allow slaves, through sheer excess of sensuous pleasure, to forget their bonds.[1] There are, however, two versions of the spiritual "Mary Had a Baby." The first references a train, which might have been the Underground Railroad.

Mary Had a Baby

Mary had a baby, Yes Lord.
Mary had a baby, yes, my Lord.
Mary had a baby, Yes Lord.
The people keep a-comin' an' de train done gone.

What did she name Him? Yes, Lord.
What did she name him? Yes, my Lord.
What did she name Him? Yes, Lord.
The people keep a-comin' an' de train done gone.

She named Him King Jesus, Yes Lord.
She named Him King Jesus, yes, my Lord.
She named Him King Jesus, Yes Lord.
The people keep a-comin' an' de train done gone.

(Available online. Suggested performer: Barbara Hendricks)

The mention of a train is significant here. In 1827, the first railroad, the Baltimore and Ohio, was chartered. It was the newest technology in existence and was extremely popular. It may account for the use of the term *railroad* in Underground Railroad since it justifies the reports of large numbers of people moving north to Canada, east to the Bahamas (Saltwater Underground Railroad), south to Florida, and west to Mexico and California, as if on a hidden railway.

The first Fugitive Slave Act was passed in 1793. It was an ordinance that left it to the states to see to the return of escaped slaves. Even this early in the history of slavery, there was discord over the laws. There were abolitionists even then, and slaves were escaping in groups and individually with their help. When they were caught, slaves fought desperately against their captors.

In 1850, Congress passed the second Fugitive Slave Act. It stated that escaped slaves in the North must be returned to their owners in the South. Slave owners quickly teamed up with bounty hunters to retrieve their "property." This went on until the Emancipation Proclamation, signed by President Lincoln in 1863, set slaves free. Information like the inception of train technology and the date of the Emancipation Proclamation helps time the appearance of the spiritual "Mary Had a Baby" from about 1830 to approximately 1865.

"Mary Had a Baby" is a call-and-response spiritual with the call being sung by a leader and the response, "Yes, Lord," being sung by the group. There are probably several versions of this song. The reason is that, as stated before, slaves learned these songs through an oral tradition. This means that depending on the memory and talent of the lead singer, the song evolved into the songs heard today. Another version of "Mary Had a Baby" is as follows:

> *Mary had a baby. Aye Lord.*
> *Mary had a baby. Aye my Lord.*
> *Mary had a baby. Mary had a baby.*
> *Mary had a baby. Aye Lord.*
>
> *What did she name him? Aye Lord.*
> *What did she name him? Aye my Lord.*
> *What did she name him? What did she name him?*
> *What did she name him? Aye Lord.*
>
> *She named him King Jesus.*
> *She named him King Jesus.*
> *She named him King Jesus. She named him King Jesus.*
> *She named him King Jesus. Aye Lord.*

(Available online. Suggested performer: Paul Robeson)

Another spiritual referencing the birth of Christ is "Go Tell It on the Mountain."

> No natural element inspired the slave poet more than the mountain, and especially the mountain top. The mountain was something he needed, rising high above the troublesome land. Although at judgment it also would flee away, it was the solidest thing he had on earth.[2]

Go Tell It on the Mountain

> *Go, tell it on the mountain,*
> *Over the hills and everywhere,*
> *Go, tell it on the mountain,*
> *That Jesus Christ was born.*

While shepherds kept their watching
O'er silent flocks by night
Behold throughout the heavens,
There shone a holy light.

Go Tell…

The shepherds feared and trembled
When, lo! above the earth
Rang out the angel chorus,
That hailed our savior's birth.

Go tell…

Down in a lowly manger
Our humble Christ was born,
And brought us all salvation,
That blessed Christmas morn.

Go tell…

(Available online. Suggested performer: Sara Evans)

One more spiritual from the life of Jesus is "He Never Said a Mumbalin' Word." It recalls the crucifixion of Jesus in graphic detail. Also dating from the end of slavery, this spiritual depicts clearly how the slave identified with the stoicism of Jesus. Slaves suffered beatings, rape, the auction block, and even being killed at the hands of a master and overseer or other white people, often without a word. In their minds, "The crucifixion [of the slave] was every bit as real as the one suffered by Jesus."[3]

He Never Said a Mumbalin' Word

They crucified my Lord, and He never said a mumbalin'
word.

They crucified my Lord, and He never said a mumbalin'
word.
Not a word, not a word, not a word.

They pierced Him in the side, and he never said a mum-
balin' word.
They pierced him in his side, and he never said a mum-
balin' word,
Not a word, not a word, not a word.

The blood came streaming down, and He never said a
mumbalin' word.
The blood came streaming down, and he never said a
mumbalin' word,
Not a word, not a word, not a word.

He hung His head and died, and He never said a mum-
balin' word.
He hung His head and died, and he never said a mum-
balin' word,
Not a word, not a word, not a word.

They laid Him in the tomb, and he never said a mum-
balin' word.
They laid Him in the tomb, and he never said a mum-
balin' word,
Not a word, not a word, not a word.

(Available online. Suggested performer: Anthony
Leon)

A familiar spiritual that alludes to the crucifixion is "Were You
There?" Sometimes referred to as a "plantation hymn," this spiritual
again speaks of the crucifixion in compelling detail. It is a tender and
beautiful hymn, the climax of its effect depending largely on the hold

and slur on the exclamation 'Oh!' with which the third line begins. It dates from the last half of the nineteenth century.

Were You There?

Were you there when they crucified my lord?
Were you there when they crucified my Lord?
Oh—Sometimes it causes me to tremble, tremble, tremble.
Were you there when they crucified my Lord?

Were you there when they nailed him to a tree?
Were you there when they nailed him to a tree?
Oh—Sometimes it causes me to tremble, tremble, tremble.
Were you there when they nailed him to a tree?

Were you there when they pierced him in his side?
Were you there when they pierced him in his side?
Oh—Sometimes it causes me to tremble, tremble, tremble.
Were you there when they pierced him in his side?

Were you there when he hung his head and died?
Were you there when he hung his head and died?
Oh—Sometimes it causes me to tremble, tremble, tremble.
Were you there when he hung his head and died?

Were you there when the sun refused to shine?
Were you there when the sun refused to shine?
Oh—Sometimes it causes me to tremble, tremble, tremble.
Were you there when the sun refused to shine?

(Available online. Suggested performer: Roland Hayes)

Few spirituals describe events in the life of Jesus because, except for Christmas (and that was not true of all slaves), slaves had to work on holidays. Christian holidays were not seen as a cause for celebration until late in the history of slavery when Christianity had become more popular among those in bondage.

---

[1] James Weldon Johnson and J. Rosamond Johnson, *American Negro Spirituals Book 2* (A Da Capo Paperback, 1969), p. 14.

[2] John Lovell *Black Song* (The Macmillan Company, 1972), p. 168.

[3] Arthur C. Jones, *Wade in the Water* (Boulder, Colorado: Leave A Little Room, 2005), p. 33.

The Underground Railroad in Code

The northern route of the Underground Railroad functioned most prominently from 1850 to the Emancipation Proclamation in 1863 and the end of the Civil War. Music played a dominant role. Many songs had double meanings, or codes, for slaves who wanted to leave the South.

One of the well-known code songs is "Follow the Drinking Gourd." There is some question as to the authenticity of the story associated with the song, but it is mentioned in most histories of spirituals.

Follow the Drinking Gourd

Follow the drinking gourd.
Follow the drinking gourd.
For the old man is-a waiting for to carry you to freedom
Follow the drinking gourd.

When the sun comes back and the first quail calls,
Follow the drinking gourd.
For the old man is-a waiting for to carry you to freedom
Follow the drinking gourd.

Follow the drinking gourd…
Well, the riverbank makes a mighty good road,
Dead trees will show you the way.
Left foot, peg foot, traveling on,
Follow the drinking gourd.

Follow the drinking gourd…

Well, where the great big river meets the little river
Follow the drinking gourd.
For the old man is-a waiting for to carry you to freedom
Follow the drinking gourd.

Follow the drinking gourd…

(Available online. Suggested performer: Richie Havens)

According to most descriptions, the drinking gourd represents the Big Dipper, where the North Star is located. So the North Star will lead one north. The first quail calls suggest that springtime is the best time to leave. Left foot, peg foot means that the singer of this song had a wooden leg, and he would leave its imprint in the mud. Where the great big river meets the little river refers to the Ohio River and one of its tributaries. Finally, the old man waiting is a man referred to as Peg Leg Joe, a man who went from plantation to plantation doing odd jobs. At each plantation he visited, he would teach this song. Slaves knew that he would meet them at the destination point and ferry them across to freedom.

Another code song is "Wade in the Water." Bounty hunters and slave owners used dogs to track runaways. This song reminded fleeing slaves that if they heard dogs barking, they should get in the water of a creek or river if they could to hide their scent and erase their footprints. This song was originally a song of baptism; it acquired its other meaning from travelers on the Underground Railroad.

Wade in the Water

Wade in the water,
Wade in the water children.
Wade in the water,
God's a gonna trouble the water.

Who's that yonder dressed in red?
God's a gonna trouble the water.
Must be the children that Moses led.
God's a gonna trouble the water.

Wade in the water…

Who's that yonder dressed in white?
God's a gonna trouble the water.
Must be the children of the Israelites.
God's a gonna trouble the waters.

Wade in the water…

Jordan's water is chilly and cold,
God's a gonna trouble the water.
Chills the body but not the soul,
God's a gonna trouble the water.

Wade in the water…

If you get there before I do,
God's a gonna trouble the water.
Tell all my friends I'm comin' too.
God's a gonna trouble the water

Wade in the water…

(Available online. Suggested performer: Sweet Honey
in the Rock)

"This Train Is Bound for Glory" is a spiritual that was also code for the Underground Railroad. It references all the things slaves despised about their slaveowners and overseers by excluding them from the band of people "bound for glory." The "train" is the group of people headed north, and "glory" is Canada, depending on when it was sung. It could have simply meant any area above the Mason-Dixon line until the 1850 Fugitive Slave Act was passed.

This Train Is Bound for Glory

This train is bound for glory, this train.
This train is bound for glory, this train.
This train is bound for glory,
Don't ride nothing but the righteous and holy,
This train is bound for glory, this train.

This train is bound for glory, this train.
This train is bound for glory, this train.
This train is bound for glory,
No hypocrites, no midnight ramblers,
This train is bound for glory, this train.

This train is bound for glory, this train.
This train is bound for glory, this train.
This train is bound for glory,
Don't ride nothing but the righteous and holy,
This train is bound for glory, this train.

(Available online. Suggested performer: Sister Rosetta Tharpe)

Short of announcing imminent plans for revolt or escape, many songs called participants to secret meetings or worship. Miles Mark Fisher, for example, has made some interesting observations about the spiritual "Let Us Break Bread Together." Fisher, pointing to the curious words, "with my face to the rising sun" notes that it is very likely that the song in its original setting "relates hardly at all to communion, which does not necessarily require early morning administration or a devotee who faces east." Rather, Fisher argues, it was employed as a signal song calling enslaved Africans to secret meetings.[1]

Let Us Break Bread Together

Let us break bread together on our knees,
Let us break bread together on our knees,
When I fall on my knees, with my face to the rising sun,
O Lord, have mercy on me.

Let us drink wine together on our knees,
Let us drink wine together on our knees,
When I fall on my knees, with my face to the rising sun,
O Lord, have mercy on me.

Let us praise God together on our knees,
Let us praise God together on our knees,
When I fall on my knees, with my face to the rising sun,
O Lord, have mercy on me.

(Available online. Suggested performer: Joan Baez)

There were probably many other code songs that offered similar information to escaping slaves, but they have not stood the test of time. The examples herein offer just a glimpse into the use of codes and signals from the Underground Railroad.

---

[1] Arthur C. Jones, *Wade in the Water* (Boulder, Colorado: Leave A Little Room, 2005), p. 49.

CHAPTER 7

More Codes, Symbols, and Masking

Sometimes credited with composing the spiritual "Steal Away,"[1] Nat Turner used it to assemble coconspirators for an 1831 insurrection in Southampton County, Virginia. Turner was a black preacher. "Centuries of reliance upon and respect for priests [in Africa] were not wiped out by American slavery. These prerogatives were merely transferred to the American preacher in their midst."[2] Nat Turner was a very religious man who held religious meetings. He was the preacher "in their midst."

With religious meetings went song, and Turner was able to use the song "Steal Away" as a code or symbol for gathering a rebellious crowd of like-minded individuals. This idea is used again and again in the Underground Railroad. The original meaning of the song continues today as a hymn, which is used in churches of various denominations.

Steal Away

Steal away, steal away,
Steal away to Jesus!
Steal away, steal away home,
I ain't got long to stay here.

My Lord calls me,
He calls me by the thunder.
The trumpet sounds within-a my soul,
I ain't got long to stay here.

Steal away, steal away,
Steal away to Jesus!
Steal away, steal away home,
I ain't got long to stay here.

(Available online. Suggested performer: the King's Singers)

"Steal Away" demonstrates the importance of the symbol of Judgment Day to African Americans as well. Referred to in several spirituals, Judgment Day is a representation of final release from bondage and oppression.

A well-known spiritual that again refers to the code or symbol of Judgment Day is "My Lord, What a Mornin'" (sometimes referred to as "My Lord, What a Mournin'"). The trumpet call is a reference in the book of Revelation in the Bible. "And I saw the seven angels which stood before God; and to them were given seven trumpets."[3] Another reference to Judgment Day states, "And the angel took the censer [a container for burning incense] and filled it with the fire of the altar, and cast it into the earth: and there were voices, and thunderings, and lightnings, and an earthquake."[4] And finally, "And the fifth angel sounded and I saw a star fall from heaven unto the earth: and to him was given the key to the bottomless pit."[5]

My Lord, What a Mornin'

My Lord, what a mornin'
My Lord, what a mornin'
My Lord, what a mornin'
When the stars begin to fall.

You'll hear the trumpet sound,
To wake the nations underground,
Look into my Lord's right hand,
When the stars begin to fall.
When the stars begin to fall.

My Lord what a mornin'
My Lord what a mornin'
My Lord what a mornin'
When the stars begin to fall.
When the stars begin to fall.

You can hear the sinner moan,
To wake the nations underground,
Look into my Lord's right hand,
When the stars begin to fall.
When the stars begin to fall.

My Lord what a mornin'
My Lord what a mornin'
My Lord what a mornin'
When the stars begin to fall.
When the stars begin to fall.

You can hear the Christians shout,
To wake the nations underground,
Look into my Lord's right hand,
When the stars begin to fall.
When the stars begin to fall.

My Lord what a mornin'
My Lord what a mornin'
My Lord what a mornin'

When the stars begin to fall
When the stars begin to fall.

(Available online. Suggested arranger: Harry T. Burleigh)

Some spirituals which reference the Day of Judgment are "In That Great Gettin' Up Mornin'"[6] and "Didn't My Lord Deliver Daniel." "Didn't My Lord Deliver Daniel" asks the following question: If the Lord delivered all these others from their misery, why shouldn't he deliver me? It was sung by Nat Turner's group of rebels and a lot of other slaves who were planning or hoping for freedom.

Didn't My Lord Deliver Daniel

Didn't my Lord deliver Daniel,
Deliver Daniel, deliver Daniel,
Didn't my Lord deliver Daniel
And why not every man?

He delivered Daniel from the lion's den
Jonah from the belly of the whale,
And the Hebrew children from the fiery furnace
And why not every man?

Didn't my Lord deliver Daniel…

The wind blows east, and the wind blows west,
It blows like the Judgement Day.
And ev'ry poor soul that never did pray
Will be glad to pray that day.

Didn't my Lord deliver Daniel…

(Available online. Suggested performer: the Nathaniel Dett Chorale)

Symbols or codes or "masks" were used in many ways. Take the spiritual "Lord, I Want to Be a Christian." The words are as follows:

Lord, I Want to Be a Christian

Lord, I want to be a Christian,
In my heart, in-a my heart,
Lord, I want to be a Christian,
In-a my heart.

Lord, I want to be more loving…

Lord, I want to be more holy…

Lord, I want to be like Jesus…

(Available online. Suggested arranger: Moses Hogan)

On the surface, the song appears to mean that there is some advantage to being a Christian, and the singers want to be involved.

> What has probably happened is that the group, as individuals, have seen a lot of people who profess Christianity and did not behave as Christians are supposed to behave…so-called Christians who go to church on Sunday morning and come home and beat their slaves on Sunday afternoon. So, using the mask of a song which seems to be praying for the Christian experience, it makes a commentary on the need for true religion, and the honest practice of the fine set of doctrines encompassed in Christianity.[7]

An example of a person being used symbolically is Pharaoh in "Oh, Mary, Don't You Weep." "Didn't Pharaoh's army get drowned" reminds the singers or listeners that if Pharaoh's army could meet their demise, so could the white people who treat them so poorly.

Oh, Mary, Don't You Weep

Oh, Mary, don't you weep, don't you mourn.
Oh, Mary, don't you weep, don't you mourn.
Didn't Pharaoh's army get drowned?
Oh, Mary, don't you weep.

Well, Mary wore three links of chain,
On each link was Jesus name
Didn't Pharaoh's army get drowned?
Oh, Mary, don't you weep.

Oh, Mary, don't you weep, don't you mourn...

(Available online. Suggested performer: Aretha Franklin)

Another reference to "Pharaoh" occurs in "Go Down, Moses." Again, with the mention of Pharaoh, slaves were confident that the white South could be overcome. The song also uses the symbol of Moses as a leader and Egypt as the South. The words of the refrain are as follows:

Go down, Moses, way down to Egypt's land.
Tell old Pharaoh to let my people go.

This collection of symbols would have a double meaning for slaves looking to escape; therefore, the use of masking, symbolism, and code in spirituals served as a call to arms. It gave African Americans an arena in which to claim their rights and point out the failings of their masters. The Bible stories from which the songs were derived provided the antagonist (i.e., Pharaoh). The power of these songs raised them above the common folksong to a place unparalleled in African or American songs alone. The spiritual became a fusion of both.

----

[1]   Others claim Wallis Willis to be the composer.
[2]   John Lovell Jr., *Black Song* (New York: The Macmillan Company, 1972), p. 31.
[3]   Revelations 8:2 KJV.
[4]   Revelations 8:5 KJV.
[5]   Revelations 9:1 KJV.
[6]   See chapter 3.
[7]   John Lovell Jr., *Black Song*, pp. 191–192.

CHAPTER 8

Florida and the Bahamas

Centuries before Harriet Tubman was born, there was an underground railroad from North to South. Florida was its earliest southerly destination. Although slavery was practiced there, it was largely wilderness. This proved a perfect venue for escaped Negroes to live undetected by potential captors.

The first slaves were brought to Florida in 1526. In 1687, Florida experienced the first emancipation of escaped slaves while Spain owned the colony. In 1735, the colony had the first settlement of free blacks. Other settlements followed, the most well-known today being Fort Mose, built in 1738. It is commonly referred to as the site of the first free black community in what is now known as the United States.

By 1738, more than one hundred freedom seekers had achieved asylum in Florida. They arrived on foot at Spanish Saint Augustine from Georgia and the Carolinas.

Abolition was not ill-thought of in the eighteenth century. Spain allowed escaped slaves freedom if they left the British plantations of Georgia and the Carolinas for Florida. Their only requirements were to recognize the Spanish Crown and adopt the Catholic religion, though men may have had to perform military service. Many from the Carolina rice plantations did just that. "Peas an' the Rice" is a work song, employed in the thrashing of rice on the floor, that likely followed escaping slaves to Florida.

Peas an' the Rice

Peas an' the rice, peas an' the rice
Peas an' the rice done, done, done. done,
Peas an' the rice, peas an' the rice done, done, done, done.
New rice an' okra, eat some an' lef' some.
Peas an' the rice, peas an' the rice done, done, done, done.

There are other spirituals connected with Florida. This song, from the movie *Twelve Years A Slave* (2013), is called "Roll, Jordan, Roll" and is known to have been sung as far south as Florida.

Roll, Jordan, Roll

Went down to the river Jordan,
Where John baptized three
Well, I walked to the devil in hell,
Sayin' John ain't baptize me. I say;

Roll, Jordan, roll.
Roll, Jordan, roll.
My soul arise in heaven, Lord,
For the year when Jordan roll

Well, some say John was a Baptist,
Some say John was a Jew,
But I say John was a preacher of God,
And my bible says so too.

Roll, Jordan, roll.
Roll, Jordan roll.

My soul arise in heaven,
For the year when Jordan roll

(Available online. Suggested performer: Topsy Chapman)

A sorrow song associated with Florida is the spiritual "My Father, How Long?" There were many large plantations along the panhandle of Florida. The rest of Florida was wilderness and beaches, not conducive to agriculture. Because of that, this song probably survives from the panhandle area in present-day Tallahassee, where most of the enslaved resided.

My Father, How Long?

My father, how long,
My father how long,
My father how long,
'Til we done sufferin' here?

My mother how long,
Oh, my mother how long,
My mother how long,
'Fore, we done sufferin' here.

And it won't be long,
And it won't be long,
And it won't be long,
The Lord will call us home.

We'll soon be free,
We'll soon be free,
We'll soon be free,
When Jesus sets me free.

We'll fight for liberty,
We'll fight for liberty,
We'll fight for liberty,
When the Lord will call us home

(Available online. Suggested performer: Various artists)

After Florida became a territory of the United States in the early nineteenth century and soon a slaveholding state, the Saltwater Underground Railroad developed. It referred to a coastal escape route along the beaches of Florida that eventually led to the Bahamas.

In 1825, Britain declared that anyone who relocated to a British territory was free, regardless of their former status. By 1834, slavery had been abolished completely in the United Kingdom and, therefore, in the Bahamas. Escaping slaves trekked from Georgia and the Carolinas as far south as Key Biscayne and found boats that would sail them the 150 miles to the Bahamas. Some even rowed their way in small boats.

The Bahamas was a desirable destination for escaped slaves because of its close distance. Resistance movements would be difficult to quell. Free blacks could marry. They could hold land. They could pursue an education. All this was an unthinkable privilege for slaves in the American South. Finally, they could easily assimilate into a population that was mostly black. Historians estimate that by the 1830s, as many as six thousand enslaved people had escaped from America to the Bahamas. Music was a part of their journey.

There is a form of celebration that was popular in the Bahamas in the late nineteenth century called the "settin' up." It usually consisted of singing all night long and was most often used for funerals. This settin' up song is a call-and-response spiritual that dates from that era. It is called "I Looked o'er Yander."

I Looked o'er Yander

I looked o'er yander; what I see?
Somebody's dying ev'ry day,

See bright angels standing dere;
Somebody's dying ev'ry day.

Ev'ry day, passin' away,
Ev'ry day, passin' away,
Ev'ry day passin' away,
Somebody's dying ev'ry day.

Hell is deep an' dark as 'spair,
Somebody's dying ev'ry day,
Stop, O sinne' don' go dere,
Somebody's dying ev'ry day.

Ev'ry day, passin' away,
Ev'ry day, passin' away,
Ev'ry day, passin' away,
Somebody's dying ev'ry day.

O come along, Moses, don' git lost!
Somebody's dying ev'ry day.
Stretch you' rod an' come acrost,
Somebody's dying ev'ry day.

Ev'ry day, passin' away,
Ev'ry day passin' away,
Ev'ry day passin' away,
Somebody's dying ev'ry day.

From the early part of the nineteenth century until the end of the Civil War in the United States, Africans escaped to the Bahamas. There, Bahamians freed many from slave ships.

In 1844, a Massachusetts sea captain, Johnathan Walker, was detained offshore in Florida with a boatload of fugitives. Walker was caught in the act of assisting runaway slaves while using the open seas

[perhaps going to the Bahamas] as an escape route…
He was branded on his right hand by a US Marshal:
the mark "S.S."—for slave stealer, a term white
southerners used as an epithet to identify those who
assisted fugitives.[1]

The following song is a shanty. A captain wanted his money
before he took on a passenger, hence the title "Pay Me My Money
Down." Contrary to popular belief, enslaved people could earn
money and were sometimes allowed to do so by their owners, though
it was very little, and they often had to buy food and clothes, pay
their masters large portions of their wages, and pay taxes on themselves. Remember, enslaved people were deemed chattel or property.
If the master deemed it proper, he could take all the slave's wages,
and many did.

Pay Me My Money Down

Pay me, Oh pay me
Pay me my money down.
Pay me or go to jail!
Pay me my money down.
Oh, pay me, Oh pay me.
Pay me my money down.
Pay me or go to jail!
Pay me my money down.

Think I heard my captain say,
Pay me my money down.
T'morrow is my sailin' day,
Pay me my money down.
(chorus)

Wish't I was Mr. Coffin's son,
Pay me my money down.

Stay in the house an' drink good rum!
Pay me my money down.
(chorus)

You owe me, pay me,
Pay me my money down.
Pay me or go to jail!
Pay me my money down.
(chorus)

Wish't I was Mr. Foster's son.
Pay me my money down.
I'd set on the bank an' see the work done.
Pay me my money down.

(Available online. Suggested performer: Bruce Springsteen)

"In the universe of southern and Caribbean plantation slaves, ships and boats were a pipeline to freedom and a refuge for slaves on the lam. Worldly and often multilingual slave sailors regularly subverted plantation discipline."[2] Soon among northern free blacks, seafaring became one of the most common male occupations. Sailing, for people of color, became an important means of making a living in the Bahamas as well.

In 1841, the commercial sponging era began and persisted into the 1930s. Sponge fishermen brought songs from slavery into the Bahamas. Because of them, there is a remnant of slave songs still in existence called the "rhyming spiritual." Rhyming spirituals were usually sung by three singers, one with a low growly voice, a lead singer (the rhymer), and one with a high, nearly falsetto voice. The rhyming spiritual does not refer to rhyme; rather, it refers to verse. The rhymer sings the couplets of the song, and the other two voices sing the response or accompaniment. "Take Me over the Tide" is a rhyming spiritual as follows:

Take Me over the Tide

I cried to the Lord, Lord, take me over the tide.
Cried to the Lord, Jesus, take me over the tide.
When my work on earth is ended and I cannot work no
     longer,
Lord, Jesus, take me over the tide.

I wanna cry to the Lord, Lord, take me over the tide.
Cried to the Lord take me over the tide.
When your work down here is ended, and you cannot
     work no longer,
Lord, Jesus, take me over the tide.

I wanna cry to the Lord, Jesus, take me over the tide.
Cried to the Lord, Take me over the tide.
When Peter was on the Sea of Galilee, reach his loving
     hand,
Said to myself, take me over the tide,

Lord, will you take me over the tide.
Cried to the Lord Jesus take me over the tide.
When my struggling days is ended Lord, you know I
     can't work no longer,
Lord, Jesus, take me over the tide.

I cried to the Lord give me the helping hand,
I cried to the Lord give me the helping hand.
When Peter was on the Sea of Galilee, reach his loving
     hand,
Lord, Jesus, take me over the tide.

(Available online. Suggested performer: see *The Real Bahamas*, volume 2)

The next shanty originated in the Bahamas also. It has African roots and was sung by fishermen in the Bahamas in the early part of the twentieth century. It's called by various names. "The Sloop John B" is one of them.

The Sloop John B

We come on the sloop John B
My grandfather and me
Around Nassau town we did roam
Drinking all night
Got into a fight,
Well, I feel so broke up,
I wanna go home.

So, hoist up the John B's sail.
See how the mainsail sets.
Call for the captain ashore,
Let me go home.
Let me go home,
I wanna go home,
Well, I feel so broke up,
I wanna go home.

The first mate, he got drunk,
And broke in the captain's trunk.
The constable had to come and take him away.
Sheriff John Stone
Why don't you leave me alone?
Well, I feel so broke up,
I wanna go home.

So, hoist up the John B sails...

The poor cook he got fits.
And threw way all my grits.

And then he took and eat up all of my corn
Let me go home.
Why don't they let me go home?
This is the worst trip I've ever been on.

So, hoist up the John B sails...

(Available online. Suggested performer: the Beach Boys)

A sorrow song often attributed to Joan Baez originated in the Bahamas as a spiritual. It is titled "All My Trials." It describes the sentiments of a dying mother comforting her children as she sings that all her trials "soon be over."

All My Trials

If religion were a thing that money could buy,
The rich would live, and the poor would die.
All my trials Lord, soon be over.

Too late my brothers,
Too late but never mind,
All my trials Lord, soon be over.
Hush little baby, don't you cry,
You know your mother was born to die,
All my trials Lord, soon be over.

(Available online. Suggested performer: Arma Lucis)

Florida was not only a haven for escaped slaves. It was also home to many enslaved African Americans, particularly in the Panhandle, on the large plantations. Songs like the ones sung in the Carolinas survived there. The Saltwater Underground Railroad developed as a passage from Florida to the Bahamas while Florida was a territory of the United States and after it became a state.

Florida joined the Union as a "slave state," and many African Americans chose to escape at that time. The closest "free" destination was the Bahamas. Upon reaching the Bahamas, the newly arrived citizens developed their own special kind of music, often shanties, work songs, or rhyming spirituals rather than the destination songs, code songs, or religious songs of the plantation.

---

[1] Catherine Clinton, *Harriet Tubman* (New York: Little, Brown and Company, 2005), p. 67.

[2] W. Jeffrey Bolster, *Black Jacks* (Cambridge, Massachusetts and London, England: Harvard University Press, 1997), p. 4.

African Americans at Sea

Often neglected in the history of slavery are African American "Blackjacks" who sailed the seas.

> Whether looking for a ship in Philadelphia, loading hogsheads of sugar into moses boats on Jamaica's north coast, sheeting home the mainsail aboard a rice-laden pettiauger on the Waccamaw River, or stewing salt beef in the smokey caboose of a London-bound tobacco ship, free and enslaved black sailors established a visible presence in every North Atlantic seaport and plantation roadstead between 1740 and 1865.[1]

Seafaring was then considered a contemptible occupation for white men, as these sailors had no personal independence, and the wages were paltry. African American slaves and freemen saw sea voyaging as an opportunity. They could see the world, and often, because of their musical skills, some acquired standing in the community. Early on, sailors who were noted for their drumming abilities would "drum up" would-be sailors for their captain by marching through the streets, assembling men near the ship to sign up for a voyage.

Musicians brought status to their masters—especially aboard privateers and naval vessels. Being assigned as musicians, a niche of notoriety if not honor, was not necessarily a liability for blacks provided they had talent.[2]

Whereas white seamen were among the most marginalized men in white society, black seamen found access to privileges, worldliness, and wealth denied to most slaves. In fact, sailors wrote the first six autobiographies of blacks published in English before 1800.

There were few black freemen on board ships in the 1700s. Slaves were the majority. There is a story of a slave from Massachusetts who, with the permission of his owner, signed up for a trip to Jamaica during the winter when the fields were frozen at home. Of course, the owner received most of his pay, but nevertheless, the slave was enjoying a summer climate.

There are shanties associated with ocean bound ships. There is one used for loading lumber, when six men on each side of the rope hauled on the block and tackle in putting a large log in place on board a vessel.[3] It is titled "Call Me Hangin' Johnny." It is a call-and-response shanty.

Call Me Hangin' Johnny

Call me hangin' Johnny.
O hang boys hang.
You call me hangin' Johnny.
O hang boys hang.
Yes, I never hang nobody.
O hang boys hang.
I never hang nobody.
O hang boys hang.
O we'll heave an' haul together.
O hang boys hang.
We heave an' haul forever.
O hang boys hang

They hang my ole grandaddy.
O hang boys hang.
They hang him for his money.
O hang boys hang.
O they hang him for his money.
O hang boys hang.
They hang him for his money.
O hang boys hang.
They call me hangin' Johnny.
O hang boys hang.
O I never hang nobody.
O hang boys hang.

(Available online. Suggested performer: Colm McGuinness Music)

Another shanty for "blocking timber" is titled "Ragged Leevy."[4]

Ragged Leevy

Ragged Leevy! Oh—Ho!
Do ragged Leevy.
Ragged Leevy! O boy!
You ragged like a jay bird!
Mr. Sipplin! Ha-n-nh,
Goin' to buil' me a sto'e fence.
In the mornin'—Oh—Ho!
Soon in the mornin',
Hos' an' buggy—Oh—Ho!
Hos' an' buggy,
Hos' an' buggy—O boy!
Dey's no one to drive 'um
Mr. Sipplin! Ha-n-nh
In de mornin',
When I rise,
I goin' to sit by de fire,

In de mornin' Oh—Ho!
O soon in de mornin',
In de mornin'
When I rise, I goin' to sit by de fire,
Mauma Dinah, Oh- Ho!
Do Mauma Dinah
Mauma Dinah.
O gal I can't suppo't you.
Mr. Sipplin! Ha-n-nh
Do Mr. Sipplin
Walkin' talkin'!
O buil' me a sto'e fence
Sweet potato Oh—Ho
Sweet potato
Sweet potato O boy.
There's two in de fire,
Mr. Sipplin'! Ha-n-nh
Goin' tto buil' me a sto'e fence
In de mornin' Oh—Ho!
When I rise, I goin' to sit by de fire.

(Available online. Suggested performance: Jake Xerxes Fussell)

Seafaring African Americans, both slaves and free, were evident from the early eighteenth century to the end of the Civil War when society changed because of emancipation. Blackjacks helped encourage the female-dominated household familiar to black Americans because sailors were away at sea so much of the time and their wives were left to take care of the home. Music accompanied these sailors, and they often were leaders in shanties.

---

1 Jeffrey Bolster, *Blackjacks*, p. 4.
2 Bolster, *Blackjacks*, p. 34.
3 Lydia Parrish, Slave Songs of the Georgia Sea Islands, p. 201.
4 Parrish, *Slave Songs*, p. 212.

Mexico and Black Seminoles

The Underground Railroad to the North promised deliverance to many of the enslaved prior to the Civil War. Some slaves of the United States escaped, not by heading north, but by crossing the southwestern border into Mexico or sailing from southern ports to Texas, which was a part of Mexico at that time.

Texas remained ambivalent about slavery and shifted from anti- to pro-stances quite often. It usually depended on whether the laws were being enforced. After independence from Spain in 1821, Mexico passed radical antislavery laws that citizens at all levels of their society were eager to enforce. This was well-known to enslaved people on the United States side of the border.[1]

William Still, Frederick Douglass, and others wrote of escape from slavery to the North, but there are few written records of southern escape, perhaps because there were so many wide-open spaces in the southwestern portion of the country. There are, however, oral traditions of both successful and attempted escapes.

There is an oral tradition of a rancher on the Rio Grande named Jackson who assisted many escaped slaves across the river by boat. Runaways knew that they could get food, clothing, and work if they wanted it.[2] A descendant of Jackson's is still living on his ranch in Texas today.

An added deterrent for escaping South was that abolitionists were not recruiting the enslaved to head to Mexico. The number of people who chose that avenue was, therefore, less than that who headed North. There were no "conductors" or "stationmasters." Repeatedly, the enslaved headed South by horse or mule, which they stole from their masters. They did not, for the most part, move in groups. Perhaps these conditions account for the lack of music found with this migration.

Also, escaped slaves who entered Mexico while it was under the rule of Spain were required to adopt the Catholic religion of Spain and, therefore, their religious music as well. Some escaping slaves chose to reach Mexico by boat, leaving from places like Galveston or New Orleans.

This shanty might refer to an escaped slave who paid passage to Mexico but was taken to Cuba instead. "Sandyanna" refers to the famous Mexican general Santa Anna who fought at the Alamo. Slaves and formerly enslaved people alike cheered for him rather than the American soldiers of their homeland.

Sandyanna

Seaman, what's the madda?
Hooray 'o-ray
Seaman, what's the madda?
Hooray, Sandy Anna.
Seaman stole my dolla'
Hooray 'o-ray
He stole it in Savannah.
Hooray, Sandy Anna,
He spend it in Havana.
Hooray 'o-ray,
I caught him in his colla'.
Hooray, Sandy Anna,
I shake 'm till he holla',
Hooray 'o-ray.

> *Seaman stole my dolla',*
> *Hooray, Sandy Anna.*

Conceivably because there were more escaped slaves in Mexico in the sixteenth and seventeenth centuries than in any other colony in the world,

> Mexicans protected fugitive slaves, just as they defended any other member of their community. In fact, during the U.S.-Mexican War, Mexican generals rallied their recruits with the rumor that the U.S. Army hoped to enslave them.

This ploy worked well for Mexico since it boasted a sizable mixed-race population.[3] There were Black Seminoles, part Native American and part African American, who lived and worked in Mexico.

The history of the Black Seminoles began in colonial times when the enslaved from the British colonies escaped into the wilderness of Florida. There, Spain abolished slavery. The escaped slaves sought refuge with Native Americans called Seminoles, who lived in Florida and knew how to navigate its swamps and jungles. They also knew how to live off the land and were willing to share their knowledge with the newly escaped slaves. The tribes and escaped slaves, who intermingled and intermarried, became known as the Black Seminoles.

Later, when Florida became a territory and then a state of the United States, slavery was reinstituted. Black Seminoles escaped across Texas into Mexico. They also escaped by ship into ports of Mexico, like Veracruz. The slaves (Negros Mascogos) were very welcome. They were warriors and often associated themselves with military outposts.

There are spirituals sung today that harken back to the period of escaping slaves. They are sung in English despite their Spanish language. These songs have adapted to their new country while retaining similar tunes and lyrics.

The first example is a new spiritual sung to an old tune: "It May Be My Last Time" is sung to a version of "Wade in the Water." The second spiritual, "Let It Shine," is a familiar set of words sung to a new tune. Both are sung by Black Seminoles living in Mexico in 2021.

It May Be My Last Time

This may be my last time,
This may be my last time,
This may be my last time,
May be my last time, I don't know
I had a mother gone before,
May be my last time, I don't know.

This may be my last time,
This may be my last time,
This may be my last time,
This may be my last time, I don't know.

I had a baby gone before,
May be my last time, I don't know.

This may be my last time,
This may be my last time,
This may be my last time,
May be my last time I don't know.

I had a father gone before,
May be my last time, I don't know.

This may be my last time,
This may be my last time,
This may be my last time,
May be my last time, I don't know.

Let It Shine

This little light of mine, I'm gonna let it shine.
This little light of mine, I'm gonna let it shine,
This little light of mine, I'm gonna let it shine,
Let it shine, let it shine, let it shine.

Don't care what you say, I'm gonna let it shine.
Don't care what you say, I'm gonna let it shine,
Don't care what you say, I'm gonna let it shine,
Let it shine, let it shine, let it shine.

This little light of mine, I'm gonna let it shine.
This little light of mine, I'm gonna let it shine,
This little light of mine, I'm gonna let it shine,
Let it shine, let it shine, let it shine.

(Available online. Suggested recording: imagine-mex-
ico.com/soul)

African music influenced Mexico's cultural history up to the
present day as documented by a radio show *Afro Pop Worldwide* titled
"La Bamba: The Afro-Mexican Story." "La Bamba" is a song popularized by Ritchie Valens in the 1950s. A folk song from Mexico,
influenced by the musical styles of Spain, Africa, and the indigenous
people of Veracruz, it is not a spiritual, shanty, or work song; it is a
dance song.

La Bamba

Para bailar la bamba
Para bailar la bamba
Se necita una poca de gracia
Una poca de gracia y otra cosita
Y arriba y arriba

Arriba y arriba y arriba ire
Por ti sere, por ti sere

Bamba, bamba
Bamba, Bamba
Bamba, bamba

Yo no soy marinero, no
Yo no soy marinero, soy capitan
Soy capitan, soy capitan

Bamba, bamba
Bamba, bamba (Bamba, bamba)
Bamba, Bamba (Bamba, bamba)
(Bamba, bamba)

Let me hear everybody now
Ah
Ah
Ah
Ah
Ah

Para bailar, bailar la bamba
Para bailar la bamba
Se necesita una poca de gracia
Y otra cosita, no

Bamba, bamba
Bamba, bamba
Bamba, bamba

Bamba, bamba
Bamba, bamba
Bamba, bamba
Bamba, bamba

Bamba, one more time
Para bailar, bailar la bamba
para bailar la bamba
Se necesita una poca de gracia
Una poca de gracia y otra cosita
Y arriba y arriba
Arriba y arriba y arriba ire
Por ti sere, por ti sere (Everybody now)

Bamba, bamba (Altogether)
Bamba, bamba (One more time)
Bamba, bamba
Bamba

(Available online. Suggested performer: Ritchie Valens)

Slaves and those protecting them while they were escaping into Mexico were every bit as passionate about their rights to freedom as their northern neighbors. Alice L. Baumgartner in her book *South to Freedom* describes several slave situations that inspired her to write her book.

She states,

> I learned about Jean Antoine, who tried to escape to Campeche in the hold of a ship and killed himself rather than return to bondage in Louisiana. I read about Manuel Luis del Fierro who threatened to shoot two slaveholders trying to kidnap a young woman named Mathilde Hennes. I came across correspondence from four town councilmen in Guerrero, Coahuila, who shot a slaveholder rather than permit him to return a runaway to the United States.[4]

There is not much music associated with these escapes, but perhaps as researchers choose to delve into the subject, more will be found.

---

1. Richard Grant, "South to the Promised Land," *Smithsonian*, vol. 53 no. 03, p. 82.
2. Grant, "South to the Promised Land," p. 81.
3. Alice Baumgartner, *South to Freedom* (New York: Basic Books, 2020), p. 179.
4. Baumgartner, *South to Freedom*, p. 255.

Abolitionists

Abolitionists played a huge role in the Underground Railroad. As mentioned earlier, Nat Turner was one, and there were many, many others. A few of them will be documented here.

William Lloyd Garrison was a crusading white publisher from Massachusetts. "I will not equivocate—I will not excuse—I will not retreat a single inch—AND I WILL BE HEARD," was his battle cry from *The Liberator* on January 1, 1831. He was thought to be too radical by some; nevertheless, he found a huge audience.

Garrison helped found the American Anti-Slavery Society in 1833. He also supported women's rights. A price was put on his head, and he was burned in effigy. Gallows were erected in front of his office at various times. Once he was put on a ship and sent to England to evade would-be assailants. There are no spirituals associated with him, though it would not be surprising if many were sung in his presence.

William Still was an abolitionist who was based in Philadelphia.

As a clerk for the Pennsylvania Society for the Abolition of Slavery...Still made numerous contacts in the abolitionist movement and quickly learned the ropes of antislavery activism. When the Society formed a General Vigilance Committee in 1852, partly in response to the notorious Fugitive Slave Act of 1850, Still was chosen to serve as secretary and then its chairman.[1]

In this capacity, he conducted regular interviews with the runaway slaves who came through Philadelphia and helped them find temporary housing. After the Civil War, he published a book that documented those arrivals. (It would have been too dangerous for runaways if he had published it before the constitutional amendment in 1867, freeing all slaves.)

A spiritual that might be associated with Still is "Children, Go Where I Send Thee!" Counting songs were occasionally used as a signal to let the stationmaster know that there were runaways seeking refuge and how many were due to arrive.

Children, Go Where I Send Thee!

Children, go where I send thee.
How shall I send thee?
I will send thee one by one,
One was the little bitty baby,
Wrapped in swaddling clothing
Lying in a manger
Born, born oh,
Born in Bethlehem.

Children, go where I send thee.
How shall I send thee?
I will send thee two by two
Two for Paul and Silas
One for the little bitty baby,
Wrapped in swaddling clothing
Lying in a manger
Born, born oh,
Born in Bethlehem.

Three for the three men riding,
Two for Paul and Silas,
One for the little bitty baby,

Four for the four who stood at the door…

Five for the gospel preachers…

Six for the six who couldn't get fixed…

Seven for the seven who went to heaven…

Eight for the eight who stood by the gate…

Nine for the nine who saw the sign…

Ten for the ten commandments…

(Available online. Suggested performer: Kenny Rogers)

John Brown was a man who chose violence to act out his abolitionist views. He was a white man who had lived in a community of free blacks in upstate New York. He fought against slavery in "Bleeding Kansas" and led a failed raid against the federal arsenal at Harpers Ferry in present-day West Virginia. He inspired some enslaved blacks to join him in the rebellion at Harpers Ferry and had support among abolitionists, even including Harriet Tubman. Harriet, along with many others, helped raise funds for the raid. It was, however, unsuccessful. Brown was hanged for treason.

Most white southerners saw Brown as insane; many white northerners and blacks saw him as a martyr. There was a song about him that many an abolitionist sang during the Civil War. "John Brown's Body" is not a spiritual; it is a camp meeting song with African American roots. Its more common text is "Battle Hymn of the Republic" by Julia Ward Howe, written well after the original.

John Brown's Body

John Brown's body lies a mouldering in the grave,
John Brown's body lies a mouldering in the grave,
John Brown's body lies a mouldering in the grave,
His soul is marching on.

Glory, glory hallelujah, Glory, glory hallelujah,
Glory, glory hallelujah, His soul is marching on.
He's gone to be a soldier in the army of our Lord,
He's gone to be a soldier in the army of our Lord
He's gone to be a soldier in the army of our Lord
His soul is marching on.
Glory, glory hallelujah, Glory, glory Hallelujah…

(Available online. Suggested performer: Pete Seeger)

Sojourner Truth, born in 1797, believed she had a special calling to travel around the country, exposing the evils of slavery. She escaped to freedom in 1826 and afterward preached abolitionism and equal rights for all. After the New York Anti-Slavery Law was passed, her former owner illegally sold her five-year-old son. With help from the Dutch Quaker couple who had bought her freedom, she went to court and won her son back. She was the first black woman to sue a white man in a US court and prevail. In the 1850s, Truth joined the women's rights movement. She helped gather supplies for black army units during the Civil War and finally worked in Kansas and Missouri to provide former slaves with property of their own.

When *Harriet Jacobs (Linda Brent)* published *Incidents in the Life of a Slave Girl* in 1861, readers were shocked by its brutality. It was her autobiography as a slave in antebellum North Carolina. Jacobs told of enslaved women with no control over whose children they bore. She described children ripped from the arms of their mothers. She recounted the violence directed against any enslaved person who dared to speak the word *no*.[2] Finally escaping the clutches of her brutal master, she hid in a tiny cubby hole under the roof of her grandmother's porch. She stayed there for seven years, coming out briefly at night. Finally, in 1842, she escaped, sailing to Philadelphia and continuing to New York City by train. There, she worked as a nurse and was reunited with her children. She remained active in African American causes until the end of her life. She even moved to Rochester, New York, and assisted Frederick Douglas with his publication of *The North Star*. "Hard Trials" might be a song that describes her situation in slavery.

Hard Trials

Been listening all the night long,
Been listening all the day,
Been listening all the night long,
For to hear some sinners pray.

Now ain't them hard trials,
Great tribulation,
Ain't them hard trials,
I'm bound to leave this land.

Oh, the foxes, they have holes in the ground,
And the birds have nests in the air,
And everything has a hiding place,
But us sinners ain't got nowhere.

Now ain't them hard trials,
Great tribulation,
Ain't them hard trials,
I'm bound to leave this land.

(Available online. Suggested performer: Marian Anderson)

Perhaps the most well-known abolitionist community was the *Quakers*. They were very active in Pennsylvania, especially

Philadelphia. They were the first religious movement to condemn slavery and prohibit members from owning slaves. They acted prominently in the escapes of thousands of slaves in the nineteenth century.

> Quaker colonists began questioning slavery in Barbados in the 1670s but first openly denounced it in 1688…The Pennsylvania Abolition Society, first founded in 1775, consisted primarily of Quakers.[3]

In the Caribbean, Africans and their descendants resisted slavery by forming communities out of white reach. They were called "*maroon societies*." In America, the *Black Seminoles* were successful in doing the same. They lived among the Native Americans, who originated in Florida. The Black Seminoles lived in separate communities and welcomed escaped slaves from South Carolina and Georgia.

There were also Black Seminoles in Oklahoma, who probably accounted for the Black Seminoles who lived in Mexico. There, they assisted Mexicans in military forays. They were very successful in that role and often lived on Mexican military bases. Today, the Black Seminoles take great pride in their history of abolition.

There were a great number of active abolitionists and abolitionist communities operating up to and through the Civil War. This chapter discussed just a few of them.

---

[1]   William Still, *The Underground Railroad*, Introduction by Ian Frederick Finseth.
[2]   American Abolitionists Knowledge Cards (New-York Historical Society).
[3]   American Abolitionists Knowledge Cards (New-York Historical Society).

Local Stationmasters

Starr Clark arrived in Mexico, New York, in 1832 and quickly became active in the abolitionist community. He was a founder of the Oswego, New York, Anti-Slavery Society and made his tin shop a meeting place for local abolitionists. According to Clark's family oral tradition, the house and the shop next door sheltered people escaping slavery. Abolitionists who met at Clark's shop aided in the following escape, one of many.

On October 1, 1851, while employed as a cooper in a shop in Syracuse, New York, an escaped slave, William "Jerry" Henry, was apprehended by authorities and was charged under the 1850 Fugitive Slave Act. During the arraignment, Jerry was able to break free and ran to a bridge over the Erie Canal where he was recaptured. A large antislavery crowd soon gathered outside the Police Justice Offices, where they were able to gain entry and free Jerry from custody. He was secreted in homes around the city, and after two weeks of hiding, he was successfully transported to Canada from Oswego, New York.

John W. Jones was born on a plantation in 1817 near Leesburg, Virginia. He was not unhappy in his situation as a slave, but when his mistress got old and began to hire out her slaves, he realized he must escape or stand on an auction block. With some friends, he escaped in 1844 to Elmira, New York. A likable chap, he soon obtained employment, married, bought a home, and took over the

Underground Railroad in the area. Elmira became the principal station between Philadelphia and Canada.

Jones worked closely with William Still, the chief Underground Railroad agent in Philadelphia, who forwarded parties of from six to ten fugitives at a time to Elmira. From Elmira, the underground forked—north, northwest, and northeast, but all routes led to Canada. Ultimately, Jones is said to have moved eight hundred slaves through Elmira to Canada.

Thomas Garrett helped more than two thousand five hundred African Americans escape slavery. He was born in 1790 in Upper Darby, Pennsylvania. His life as an abolitionist began when a free black woman who worked for the Garretts was kidnapped by slave traders intending to sell her into the Deep South. Garrett rescued her and was determined to defend African Americans throughout his life.

Garrett endeavored openly as a stationmaster when he moved to Wilmington, Delaware. He worked closely with William Still and was a friend and benefactor to Harriet Tubman. He was the inspiration for Harriet Beecher Stowe's abolitionist character, Simeon Halliday, in her famous novel, *Uncle Tom's Cabin.* As was Garrett, Simeon was unafraid of risking fines or imprisonment for helping his fellow man.[1]

Levi Coffin was a Quaker abolitionist who, with his wife, Catherine, helped more than two thousand enslaved people escape to freedom. He was an active leader of the Underground Railroad in Indiana and Ohio. He was a director of a bank, and with his financial position and standing in the community, he helped supply food, clothing, and transportation for the Underground Railroad in the region.

Coffin assisted hundreds of runaway slaves by lodging them in his Ohio home, across the river from Kentucky and not far from Virginia. Both Kentucky and Virginia remained slave states until slavery was abolished after the Civil War.[2]

Samuel D. Burris was a free black man who was born in Delaware but moved his family to Philadelphia. From there, he traveled into

Maryland and Delaware to guide freedom seekers North, along the Underground Railroad to Pennsylvania.

In 1847, after helping several enslaved Africans, he was arrested for enticing escaped slaves to run away. He was found guilty and was put on the auction block to be sold into slavery. When abolitionists found out that Burris was about to be sold, Isaac Flint posed as a slave buyer, bought him, and set him free.

Burris still went into Delaware to guide freedom seekers until a law was passed that said that anyone who helped him would receive sixty lashes and be sold into slavery. He and his family moved to San Francisco, where he raised funds for education, food, and shelter for former slaves. He also helped freed people become established with jobs and homes.

The above stationmasters represent hundreds of people, both African American and white, who assisted escaping slaves in many ways and places throughout the country. For African Americans, their lives and often their freedom were at risk, and whites faced hideous ridicule and enormous fines. All were heroes in the fight against slavery.

---

[1]   American Abolitionists Knowledge Cards (New-York Historical Society).
[2]   American Abolitionists Knowledge Cards (New-York Historical Society).

Spirituals without Codes

Countless spirituals were generated beyond the scope of the Underground Railroad. Some are cheerful and even boisterous. Sometimes, they helped stir people into a frenzy of spiritual exuberance. People would sing and dance in excess. Such is the spiritual "Gonna Sing When the Spirit Says Sing." There would be accompaniment of hand clapping and stomping of feet. It might even have turned into a ring shout.

Gonna Sing When the Spirit Says Sing

Gonna sing when the spirit says sing!
Gonna sing when the spirit says sing!
Gonna sing when the spirit says sing!
And obey the spirit of the Lord.

Gonna shout when the spirit says shout!…

Gonna pray when the spirit says pray!…

(Available online. Suggested performer: West Village Chorale)

"Lonesome Valley" is sometimes referred to as a "white spiritual," but John Lovell Jr. describes it as an African American spiritual. Once one had done all he could for himself and had set his heart in the right direction, then he could reach out to the Powers that Be for help.

Lonesome Valley

Oh, you got tuh walk-a that lonesome valley,
You got tuh walk it by yo'sef,
No one heah to go tha with you,
You got tuh go tha by yo'sef.

Jordon's stream is cold and chilly,
You got tuh wade it faw yo'sef,
Nos one heah tuh wade it faw you,
You got tuh wade it by yo'sef.

When my dear Lawd was hangin' bleedin'
He had tuh hang tha by his-sef,
No one tha could hang tha for Him
He had tuh hang tha by his-sef.
When you reach the rivah Jurdun,
You got tuh cross it by yo'sef,
No one heah may cross it with you,
You got tuh cross it by yo'sef.

When you face that judgemunt mawnin'
You got tuh face it by yo'sef,
No one heah tuh face it faw you,
You got tuh face it by yo'sef

You got tuh stan' yo' trial in judgemunt,
You go tuh stan' it by yo'sef,

No one heah tuh stan' it faw you,
You got tuh stan' it by yo'sef.

(Available online. Suggested performer: Pete Seeger/
Arlo Guthrie)

An exalted rendering of a spiritual is "Ride On, King Jesus."
Jesus in some songs was portrayed as a companion or leader in battle.
One of the most majestic musical affirmations of Jesus's leadership
was this spiritual.[1] Although there is no reference to the Underground
Railroad, there is a powerful statement of the slave's resistance to
bondage.

Ride On, King Jesus

Ride on, King Jesus,
No man can-a hinder me
Ride on, King Jesus
No man can-a hinder me.

I was young when I begun,
No man can-a hinder me
But now my race is almost done,
No man can-a hinder me.

(Available online. Suggested arranger: Moses Hogan)

In this song, we can feel the resolve of generations of
African Americans who have used it to bolster their
persistent ride on the road to freedom…In singing
and dancing this song, we can be sure that each par-
ticipant felt, with complete determination, "no man
can-a hinder me!"[2]

Deliverance is the theme of many spirituals. Such is the case of "There Is a Balm in Gilead." It answers Jeremiah 8:22 in the Bible when the prophet asks, "Is there no balm in Gilead?"

There Is a Balm in Gilead

There is a balm in Gilead,
To make the wounded whole,
There is a balm in Gilead,
To heal the sin-sick soul.

Sometimes I feel discouraged,
And think my work's in vain,
But then the Holy Spirit
Revives my soul again.

There is a balm in Gilead...

Don't ever feel discouraged,
For Jesus is your friend,
And if you lack for knowledge,
He'll not refuse to lend.

There is a balm in Gilead...

If you cannot preach like Peter,
If you cannot pray like Paul,
You can tell the love of Jesus
And say, "He died for all."

There is a balm in Gilead...

(Available online. Suggested performer: Chanticleer)

Many spirituals reference coming events. Sometimes they are even a call to arms. "Great Day! Great Day the Righteous Marching" is that kind of spiritual.

Great Day! Great Day the Righteous Marching

Great day! Great day the righteous marching;
Great day! God's gonna build up Zion's walls!
Great day! Great day the righteous marching;
Great day! God's gonna build up Zion's walls!

Chariot rode on the mountain top,
God's gonna build...
My God spoke and the chariot did stop,
God's gonna build...

Great day! Great day the righteous marching...

This is the day of jubilee,
God's gonna build...
The lord has set His people free,
God's gonna build...

Great day! Great day the righteous marching...

We want no cowards in our band,
God's gonna build...
We call for valiant-hearted men,
God's gonna build...

Great day! Great day the righteous marching...

Goin't take my breastplate, sword and shield,
God's gonna build...
And march out boldly in the field,
God's gonna build...

Great day! Great day the righteous marching…

(Available online. Suggested performer: Howard University Choir)

Although the enslaved might not have been interested in inter-marriage, they were certainly integrationists on the grounds that anything less was degrading and insulting. To be denied the ordinary treatment exacted of human beings was unbearable to them.[3] Poetic rendering of this philosophy was expressed in the spiritual "I'm Gonna Sit at the Welcome Table."

I'm Gonna Sit at the Welcome Table

I'm gonna sit at the welcome table;
I'm gonna sit at the welcome table, one of these days.
I'm gonna sit at the welcome table;
Gonna sit at the welcome table, one of these days.

I'm gonna eat and drink with my Jesus;
I'm gonna eat and drink with my Jesus, one of these days.
I'm gonna eat and drink with my Jesus;
Gonna eat and drink with my Jesus, one of these days.

I'm gonna join with my sisters and brothers;
I'm gonna join with my sisters and brothers, one of these days
I'm gonna join with my sisters and brothers;
Gonna join with my sisters and brothers one of these days.

All the world will find a welcome;
All the world will find a welcome one of these days.
All the world will find a welcome;
All the world will find a welcome, one of these days.

We'll feast on milk and honey;
We'll feast on milk and honey, one of these days.

We'll feast on milk and honey;
Gonna feast on milk and honey one of these days.

(Available online. Suggested performer: Courtney Patton)

"Deep River" is a spiritual that describes the yearning of a slave for "the promised land," which could mean either earthly freedom or heaven. It uses many code words; however, it was popularized in 1916 when Harry T. Burleigh wrote an arrangement of it. It is unlikely that it was an Underground Railroad song.

Deep River

Deep river, my home is over Jordan.
Deep river Lord, I want to cross over into campground.

Oh, don't you want to go to that gospel land?
That promised land, where all is peace.

Deep River, my home is over Jordan.
Deep river, I want to cross over into campground.

(Available online. Suggested performer: Marian Anderson)

These spirituals each represent an individual take on subjects that are common among African American songs. Whether they are boisterous or peaceful, a call to arms or a call to sit at the welcome table, they each portray the slave as a poet and person who is unwilling to accept his bondage any longer.

---

[1] Arthur C. Jones, *Wade in the Water* (Boulder, Colorado: Leave A Little Room, 2005), p. 58.

[2] Jones, *Wade in the Water*, p. 58.

[3] John Lovell Jr. *Black Song: The Forge and the Flame* (New York: The Macmillan Company, 1972), p. 227.

The Development and Evolution of Spirituals

There are basically three stages of development in the spiritual. An example of the first stage, "You May Bury Me in the East," is, according to W. E. B. Du Bois, nearly pure African music.

You May Bury Me in the East

You may bury me in the east,
You may bury me in the west,
But I'll hear the trumpet sound.
In-a that morning
In-a that morning, my Lord
How I long to go,
For to hear that trumpet sound
In-a that morning.

In that dreadful judgement day
We'll take wings and fly away,
But I'll hear that trumpet sound.
In-a that morning.
How I long to go,

For to hear that trumpet sound
In-a that morning.

Good old Christians, in that day
We'll take wings and fly away,
For to hear that trumpet sound.
In-a that morning, my Lord
How I long to go
For to hear that trumpet sound,
In-a that morning.

(Available online. Suggested performers: Fisk Jubilee Singers)

"Jacob's Ladder" exemplifies the second stage. At its inception, spirituals had become more African American. Composed in the early eighteenth century, it describes a weary climb out of degradation. It has some mild syncopation and an Old Testament Bible story.

Jacob's Ladder

We are climbing Jacob's ladder,
We are climbing Jacob's ladder,
We are climbing Jacob's ladder,
Soldiers of the cross.

Ev'ry round goes higher, higher,
Ev'ry round goes higher, higher,
Ev'ry round goes higher, higher,
Soldiers of the cross.

Children, do you love my Jesus?
Children, do you love my Jesus?
Children, do you love my Jesus?
Soldiers of the cross.

If you love Him, why not serve Him?

Rise, shine, give God glory…

(Available online. Suggested performer: Paul Robeson)

The third stage incorporates more of the Colonial American music slaves heard. One example is "I Hope My Mother Will Be There on High." It is strongly influenced by the gospel music of the camp meeting.

I Hope My Mother Will Be There on High

I hope my mother will be there,
In that beautiful world on high,
That used to join with me in pray'r.
In that beautiful world on high.

Oh, I will be there, Oh I will be there,
With the Palms of victory,
Crowns of glory you shall wear,
In that beautiful world on high.

I hope my sister will be there,
In that beautiful world on high,
That used to join with me in pray'r,
In that beautiful world on high.

Oh, I will be there, Oh I will be there…

I hope my brother will be there,
In that beautiful world on high,
That used to join with me in pray'r,
In that beautiful world on high.

Oh, I will be there, Oh I will be there…

I know my Savior will be there,
In that beautiful world on high,
That used to listen to my pray'r,
In that beautiful world on high.

Oh, I will be there, Oh I will be there…

(Available online. Suggested performer: Kirk Ward)

No one knows exactly how spirituals were originally composed. There were, in Africa, figures called griots, who were storytellers, or more often songsmiths, who oversaw the imparting of history in each village, musically. "Their job was to mentally record and transmit ancestral lineage, customs, beliefs, events, names, dates, and legends from generation to generation. The griots learned and taught via an oral tradition, based on memory."[1] It could be that the tradition of the griot, if not the village, continued in the United States. In any case, there were talented slaves on every plantation who were able to improvise and lead or compose songs.

Songs evolved and were spread in many ways. Slaves, imported from different parts of the country, brought their songs with them. The most likely migration was by way of the auction block. Usually, slaves who had tried to escape were auctioned off. Often slaves were sold to settle an estate. Slaves could be sold for any reason, and they took their music with them to their new plantation.

Praise houses, which came into being later in slavery, offered another means for sharing music. They were community houses built by slaves for gatherings. Often built despite the masters' opposition, they provided a space where slaves could celebrate or work together. "Communal gatherings such as baptisms, or funerals, or corn shucking offered these types of opportunities."[2] There was always music.

Christmas week was a tradition in the South among slaveholders. There was leniency for a week. Slaves could visit other plantations at will. They were given lots of whiskey, and there was plenty of room for debauchery. This provided a means for the slaveholder to redeem himself in the eyes of the slaves. An owner could feel more comfortable in his role as a persecutor. Music was an integral part of these visits and was shared from plantation to plantation.

Another way music evolved was on boats or ships. Early in the history of slavery, there were many enslaved sailors and watermen. Sailors traversed the seas and brought bits of music from all over the world back to America. Watermen paddled the rivers, canals, and shoreline. An example of a river song is "Do, Lord, Remember Me," which, according to John Lovell Jr., was sung on a ferry crossing between Saint Helena and Beaufort, South Carolina.

Do Lord, Remember Me

Do Lord, oh do Lord, oh do remember me.
Do Lord, oh do Lord, oh do remember me.
Do Lord, oh do Lord, oh do remember me.
Look away beyond the blue.

I've got a home in Glory Land that outshines the sun.
I've got a home in Glory Land that outshines the sun.
I've got a home in Glory Land that outshines the sun.
Look away beyond the blue.

Do Lord, oh do Lord, oh do remember me…

I took Jesus as my Savior; you take him too.
I took Jesus as my Savior; you take him too.
I took Jesus as my Savior; you take him too.
Look away beyond the blue.

Do Lord, oh do Lord, oh do remember me…

(Available online. Suggested performer: Mississippi John Hurt)

European music was also an influence on spirituals. Sometimes slaves were required to go to a white church and sit outside or in the back. They heard the music of the "white folks" and assimilated it into their songs. Later, camp meetings became popular. They were integrated; often blacks and whites listened to the same preacher but were separated from one another. So camp meetings and churches operated as a melting pot for the evolution of these songs.

Spirituals developed and evolved through slaves' contact with enslaved from different places, particularly different plantations, communal gatherings in the praise houses, Christmas gatherings, attendance at white churches, and later, camp meetings. Camp meetings were integrated to some extent and provided an opportunity to hear new songs. Watermen or African American sailors brought a rich assortment of music to America's shores as well. All these influences contributed to the development and evolution of spirituals.

---

[1]   Tobin and Dobard, *Hidden in Plain View*, p. 37.
[2]   Guenther, *In Their Own Words*, p. 13.

C H A P T E R 1 5

Styles of Spirituals

There are basically three styles of spirituals.[1] The most prevalent examples are the "Call-and-Response" spirituals. They have a singer who is the leader and sings the call and a group that sings the response or refrain.

> Call-and-Response was a practical approach in an oral, non-literate society. It was also handy in a work song which might go on for hours and hours as the slaves labored. It provided the built-in "extendibility" they needed when grinding grain, spinning, weaving, working in the field, all activities accompanied by singing.[2]

Call and response were useful to slaves as they provided the singers with a set format. All a leader had to do was change a word or a phrase, and the group would respond, usually with the same refrain. A fine example of a call-and-response spiritual is "Somebody's Knocking at Your Door."

Somebody's Knocking at Your Door

Somebody's knocking at your door.
Somebody's knocking at your door.

Oh, sinner, why don't you answer?
Somebody's knocking at your door.

Knocks like Jesus
Somebody's knocking at your door
Knocks like Jesus.
Somebody's knocking at your door.
Oh, sinner, why don't you answer?
Somebody's knocking at your door.

Can't you hear him?
Somebody's knocking at your door.
Can't you hear him?
Somebody's knocking at your door.
Oh, sinner, why don't you answer?
Somebody's knocking at your door.

Somebody's knocking at your door.
Somebody's knocking at your door.
Oh, sinner, why don't you answer?
Somebody's knocking at your door.

(Available online. Suggested performer: OCP Session Choir)

The second style of spirituals is characterized by long slow phrases. Often sorrow songs, they are generally descriptions of the pain and suffering the enslaved are experiencing. This example, "Calvary," describes the pain and suffering of Jesus on the cross. The figure of Jesus resonated with enslaved people.

Calvary

Calvary, Calvary,
Calvary, Calvary,

Calvary, Calvary,
Truly He died on Calvary.

Don't you hear that clamoringin'?
Don't you hear that clamoringin'?
Don't you hear that clamoringin'?
Truly He died on Calvary.

Calvary, Calvary,
Calvary, Calvary,
Calvary, Calvary,
Truly He died on Calvary.

(Available online. Suggested arranger: Moses Hogan)

The third musical style is driven more by rhythm than by melody.[3] The tempo is quick, and contrary to the second style, it gives the singers and listeners a lift rather than an account of the wrongs that have befallen them. "I Got Shoes" is an example of this style.

I Got Shoes

I got shoes, you got shoes,
All of God's children's got shoes
When I get to heaven gonna put on my shoes,
I'm gonna walk all over God's heaven, heaven
Everybody talkin' bout heaven ain't goin' there
Heaven, heaven
Gonna walk all over God's heaven.

I got wings, you got wings,
All of God's children's got wings.
When I get to heaven gonna put on my wings
I'm gonna fly all over God's heaven, heaven
Everybody talkin' bout heaven ain't goin' there,

Heaven, heaven
I'm gonna fly all over God's heaven.

I got a crown, you got a crown,
All of God's children's got a crown,
When I get to heaven gonna put on my crown
I'm gonna shine all over God's heaven, heaven
Everybody talkin' bout heaven ain't goin' there
Heaven, heaven
I'm gonna shine all over God's heaven

I got a harp, you got a harp,
All of God's children's got a harp.
When I get to heaven gonna play on my harp,
I'm gonna play all over God's heaven, heaven
Everybody's talkin' bout heaven ain't goin' there,
Heaven, heaven,
I'm gonna play all over God's heaven.

(Available online. Suggested performer: Marian Anderson)

These three styles of spirituals don't necessarily exemplify every spiritual. Toward the end of slavery, when spirituals were evolving into gospel, gospel often predominated and didn't necessarily fit these categories, but for the traditional spiritual, "call and response," "long slow phrases," and "driven by rhythm" are authentic descriptions.

---

[1] Guenther, *In Their Own Words*, p. 31.
[2] Guenther, p. 31.
[3] Guenther, p. 32.

C H A P T E R   1 6

Religion and Slavery in the South

"Slaves prayed face down to prevent the sound carrying. When slaves wanted to sing or pray, they had to steal into the woods. If heard singing and praying, they were whipped all the way home."[1]

O I Couldn't Hear Nobody Pray

O I couldn't hear nobody pray
O I couldn't hear nobody pray,
Way down yonder by myself,
I couldn't hear nobody pray.

In the valley,
O I couldn't hear nobody pray
On my knees,
O I couldn't hear nobody pray
With my burden,
O I couldn't hear nobody pray
And my Savior
O I couldn't hear nobody pray
O my Lord,

O I couldn't hear nobody pray…

Chilly waters,
O I couldn't hear nobody pray
In the Jordan,
O I couldn't hear nobody pray
Crossing over,
O I couldn't hear nobody pray
Into Canaan,
O I couldn't hear nobody pray
O my Lord
O I couldn't hear nobody pray
Hallelujah
O I couldn't hear nobody pray,
Troubles over
O I couldn't hear nobody pray,
In the Kingdom
O I couldn't hear nobody pray
With my Jesus
O I couldn't hear nobody pray
O my Lord

O I couldn't hear nobody pray…

(Available online. Suggested performer: Jessye Norman)

"To begin with, blacks retained much of the African's tendency to consider religion as a totality, a unifying element in his life. This fact alone would prevent his swallowing whole the religious views of his masters, even if the masters had consistently imparted them to him."[2] However, as they began to assimilate the culture and learn the language, the enslaved acquired an affinity for Christianity. Owners considered slaves heathens, and many wanted to convert them. In fact, it was one of the ways owners justified slavery.

At first, slaves were attracted to the Old Testament stories in the Bible. Later, they accepted the entire Bible wholeheartedly. Among the early spirituals was perhaps "Ezekiel Saw the Wheel." It is an Old Testament reference, and though the first verse remains consistent in all the performances of the spiritual, the various later renditions incorporate the New Testament into the final verses.

Ezekiel Saw the Wheel

Ezekiel saw that wheel,
Way up in the middle of the air,
Ezekiel saw that wheel,
Way up in the middle of the air.

Now the little wheel runs by faith,
And the big wheel runs by the grace of God,
And a wheel in a wheel whirling,
Way up in the middle of the air.

Tell you what a hypocrite he will do,
Way up in the middle of the air,
He'll talk about me, he'll talk about you,
Way up in the middle of the air.

Ezekiel saw that wheel…

Brothers and sisters tell you what you gotta do,
Way up in the middle of the air,
Join about union two by two,
Way up in the middle of the air.

Ezekiel saw that wheel…

Tell you what a bootlegger he will do,
Way up in the middle of the air,
Sell you liquor and liquor with fruit,
Way up in the middle of the air.

Ezekiel saw that wheel…

(Available online. Suggested arranger: W. L. Dawson)

During the Great Awakening, a religious revitalization dating from the 1730s to 1750s (depending on the plantation), some owners, or more often the owners' wives, would take their slaves aside on Sunday and teach them about religion. They might have also taken them to church where slaves would hear sermons, instructing them to be obedient and not to steal. The enslaved did not enjoy these sermons; however, they did receive good preaching from their own enslaved preachers either in secret or later in praise houses located on the plantation.

Slaves were ultimately allowed black ministers to "sermonize" them, but the black preachers toed the line, so there wasn't much difference between their own preachers and white preachers. Owners endorsed Presbyterian and Episcopal churches with their slaves because their music was not particularly exuberant. Slaves appreciated lively music they could dance and clap to, like that of the Methodists and Baptists of the time.

With the second Great Awakening (1795–1835) came the advent of camp meetings. They were revivals that included an emotionally charged conversion of the heart, rooted in initiation rituals of Africa, combined with ecstatic actions of shouting, dancing, clapping, and singing. They were produced largely by Methodists, and slave music was strongly influenced by these affairs. Revivals continued well past the era of Emancipation. Among the spirituals that might have been sung at such an event was "Give Me That Old Time Religion."

Give Me That Old Time Religion

Give me that old time religion,
Give me that old time religion,
Give me that old time religion,

It's good enough for me.
It was good for our mothers,
It was good for our mothers,
It was good for our mothers,
It's good enough for me.

Give me that old time religion…

Makes me love everybody
Makes me love everybody,
Makes me love everybody,
It's good enough for me.

Give me that old time religion…

It will take us all to heaven,
It will take us all to heaven,
It will take us all to heaven,
It's good enough for me.

Give me that old time religion…

(Available online. Suggested performer: The Plantation Singers)

Sunday prayer meetings in the quarters could, if allowed to, last all day. They were lively affairs as can be demonstrated by this quote from a former slave:

> On Sundays they had meetin', sometimes at our house, sometimes at 'nother house…They'd preach and pray and sing—shout, too. I heard them git up with a powerful force of the spirit, clappin' they hands and walkin' round the place. They'd shout, "I got that old time 'ligion in my heart."[3]

Slaves on some plantations would be allowed to work for wages in their spare time. They would buy Sunday clothes with their money and were proud of their appearance. However, some slaves had only one or two outfits per year. Certainly, those people could not dress up for church even if they were allowed to go.

After Emancipation, churches remained the foundation of the community. Former slaves were eager to learn to read and write. There were no schools available to them, and churches provided a place for that. Churches took on the role of communal gathering places at that time and maintained it well into the twentieth century.

Religious format varied from plantation to plantation. Some owners allowed religion on the plantation. Others would take their slaves to church. Some did not permit any form of religion at all. Despite this, Christianity thrived among slaves and former slaves in the Americas, and the church was a mainstay in the African American community well into the twentieth century.

---

[1]   Lovell, *Black Song*, p. 183.

[2]   Lovell, p. 181.

[3]   Albert J. Raboteau, *Slave Religion: The "Invisible Institution" in the Antebellum South* (Oxford, New York, Toronto, Melbourne: Oxford University Press, 1980), p. 221.

Artists Who Helped Popularize the Spiritual

Marian Anderson (1897–1993) had a remarkable voice even as a child. All the while she was growing up, she sang for her church and other churches in her hometown of Philadelphia, Pennsylvania. When she graduated from high school, she went to a music school to apply. They would not consider her because she was black. She went to a teacher and studied privately. Soon, she was singing with the New York Philharmonic and even at Carnegie Hall. She was determined to study opera. With the help of her church and family, she went to Europe and was able to accomplish her goal. She toured Europe for several years and finally returned home to Philadelphia in 1937 as an international diva.

People all over the world wanted to hear Anderson sing, especially in America, but there was no venue to accommodate the numbers who wanted to attend. Her manager requested the use of Constitution Hall in Washington, DC, but was refused because she was black. Finally, after a long search, President Franklin D. and Eleanor Roosevelt intervened, and Marian sang in front of the Lincoln Memorial. Seventy-five thousand people of every race and color went to hear the concert. "He's Got the Whole World in His Hands" is the song title in one of her albums.

He's Got the Whole World in His Hands

He's got the whole world in his hands,
He's got the whole world in his hands,
He's got the whole world in his hands,
He's got the whole world in his hands.

He's got the little bitty baby in his hands…
He's got the whole world in his hands.

He's got the whole world in his hands…

He's got you and me brother in his hands,
He's got you and me sister in his hands,
He's got you and me brother in his hands,
He's got the whole world in his hands.
He's got the whole world in his hands [4X]

(Available online. Suggested performer: Marian Anderson)

Paul Robeson (1898–1976) was an African American athlete, lawyer, singer, and actor who lived through some of the worst racial discrimination in America. He was born in 1898 to a runaway slave who also managed to graduate from Lincoln University and a mother from a Quaker abolitionist family. Their life was not easy. Robeson often performed spirituals and is known to have sung songs of protest in twenty-five different languages. Despite the Emancipation Proclamation, he knew from sad experience that African Americans were anything but equal.

Racism, rampant in America, was not the same in Europe. He performed in England to as many as ten or twelve standing ovations. His performances in America were met with threats and harassment. He spoke out against racism anyway, worked for the rights of labor, and advocated for peace. His passport was revoked at one point but was returned to him, after which he toured Australia and

New Zealand to standing-room-only crowds. He died in 1976 in Philadelphia, Pennsylvania. "No More Auction Block for Me" is a spiritual, one of many that he recorded.

No More Auction Block for Me

No more auction block for me,
No more, no more,
No more auction block for me,
Many thousand gone.

No more pint of salt for me,
No more, no more,
No more pint of salt for me,
Many thousand gone.

No more driver's lash for me,
No more, no more,
No more driver's lash for me,
Many thousands gone.

(Available online. Suggested performer: Paul Robeson)

Fisk University Jubilee Singers were the first to popularize the spiritual. Fisk opened its doors in January 1866 as a high school and eventually developed into a college and normal school, providing one of the first places of training for African American elementary school teachers.

The beginning years of Fisk University were difficult, and the school was constantly struggling for funds to remain open. A music teacher on the faculty, George White, suggested a concert tour of students to raise funds. Although his suggestion was met with resistance, he proceeded anyway.

Their original program did not include spirituals, although they sang them in the chapel. The students who were in the choir resisted the idea as all the members except one had been born into slavery and didn't expect a welcome from their white listeners. Nevertheless, spirituals became the subject of their concerts. Arthur C. Jones in his book *Wade in the Water* described an event in Oberlin, Ohio, as the turning point. John Lovell Jr. describes a much longer process in his book *Black Song*. The Jubilee Singers contributed greatly to the emerging worldwide appeal and influence of spirituals. "I Got A Home Up In-a Dat Rock" is a spiritual sung by the Jubilee Singers.

I Got a Home Up in-a Dat Rock

I got a home in-a dat rock, don't you see?
I got a home in-a dat rock, don't you see?
Between the earth and sky,
I thought I heard my Savior cry,
You got a home in-a dat rock, don't you see?

Poor man Lazarus poor as I, don't you see?
Poor man Lazarus poor as I, don't you see?
Poor man Lazarus poor as I,
When he died, he got a home on high,
He got a home in-a dat rock, don't you see?

Rich man died as he lived so well, don't you see?
Rich man died as he lived so well, don't you see?
Rich man died as he lived so well,
And when he died, he got a home in Hell,
He had no home in-a dat rock, don't you see?

God gave Noah the rainbow sign, don't you see?
God gave Noah the rainbow sign, don't you see?
God gave Noah the rainbow sign,
No more water but fire next time,
Better get a home in-a dat rock, don't you see?

(Available online. Suggested performer: Fisk Jubilee Singers)

Mahalia Jackson (1911–1972) was most famous as a gospel singer but was known for her interpretation of spirituals as well. She was born in New Orleans, and although her grandparents had been slaves, she was educated in New Orleans public schools. Because she was brought up in churches where the people sang a great many spirituals, when she first sang in public, she sang "Standin' in the Need of Prayer." Like most successful singers of spirituals, she was deeply sincere about them and believed strongly in the message they carry.[1]

Standin' in the Need of Prayer

Not my brother, not my sister, but it's me, O lord,
Standin' in the need of prayer,
Not my brother, not my sister, but it's me, O Lord,
Standin' in the need of prayer.

It's me, it's me, it's me, O Lord,
Standin' in the need of prayer,
It's me, it's me, it's me, O Lord,
Standin' in the need of prayer.

Not the preacher, not the deacon, but it's me, O Lord…

It's me, it's me, it's me, O Lord…

Not my father, not my mother, but it's me, O Lord…

It's me, it's me, it's me, O Lord…

Not the stranger, not my neighbor, but it's me, O Lord…

It's me, it's me, it's me, O Lord…

(Available online. Suggested performer: John Clayton Jazz [instrumental])

Harry T. Burleigh (1866–1949) is credited with having done more than anyone else to prepare spirituals for the concert stage, both for individuals and ensembles. Not only were his arrangements used by many black artists like Marian Anderson and Paul Robeson, but they were also used by white performers. Discrimination being what it was at the time, many white performers dropped the arrangements from their programs when they discovered that the arranger was African American. Conservatory trained, he knew the composer Antonin Dvorak personally and strongly influenced him in several of his compositions. His arrangements are still used today in concert performances. One of his popular arrangements is "Ev'ry Time I Feel the Spirit."

Ev'ry Time I Feel the Spirit

Ev'ry time I feel the spirit movin' in my heart, I will
    Pray.
Ev'ry time I feel the spirit movin' in my heart, I will
    pray.

Upon the mountain, when my Lord Spoke
Out of his mouth came fire and smoke.
I looked around me, it looked so fine,
Till I asked my Lord if all were mine.

Ev'ry time I feel the spirit…

Jordan River, is chilly and cold,
it chills the body, but not the soul.
There is but one train upon this track,
It runs to heaven and then right back.

Ev'ry time I feel the spirit…

(Available online. Suggested arranger: Burleigh)

Odetta (1930–2008) was known mostly for her folk singing, but her repertoire consisted of American folk music, blues, jazz, and spirituals. In 1963, at a civil rights demonstration, she sang "O Freedom." She was very involved in both theater and musical theater. She received three Grammy Awards and many other awards as well. Remembered for her renderings of "This Little Light of Mine" and "Sometimes I Feel Like a Motherless Child," she also recorded two albums of Christmas spirituals. The following is a spiritual from one of those recordings.

Ain't That A-rocking?

Mary had a little baby,
Wrapped in swaddling clothes,
Every time the little baby cried,
She'd rock him in a weary land.

Ain't that a-rocking all night,
All night long
Ain't that a-rocking all night,
All night long
Ain't that a-rocking all night,
All night long

Wise men came from the east,
Guided by a star,
With gold, myrrh and frankincense
While she rocked him in a weary land

Herod heard the news,
The baby he did seek,
The Lord told Mary,
Just you rock him in a weary land.

(Available online. Suggested artist: Odetta)

Harry Belafonte (1927–2023) was a singer, activist, and artist. One of his best-known recordings is "Jamaica Farewell." He recorded in many genres, including blues, folk, gospel, show tunes, and American standards. He considered Paul Robeson a mentor and was a close confidant of Martin Luther King Jr. He won three Grammy Awards (one a Lifetime Achievement Award) as well as numerous other awards and recognitions. Sung at the funeral of his friend, Sidney Poitier, "Amen, Amen, Amen" is a well-known spiritual.

Amen, Amen, Amen

Amen, amen, amen, amen, amen
Amen, amen, amen, amen, amen.

See the little baby,
Lyin' in the manger
On Christmas mornin'

See him in the temple,
Talkin' to the elders
How they marveled at his wisdom.

Amen, amen…

(Available online. Suggested performer: Moses Hogan Singers)

Kathleen Battle (1948–) is an operatic soprano. She began her career as a music teacher for fifth and sixth graders, but two years after that, she began her professional singing career. Throughout the 1980s, she performed in recitals and choral works and became an established artist at the Metropolitan Opera Company in New York. During this time, she received three Grammys. She recorded a CD of spirituals in the 1990s and performed a concert of spirituals with Jessye Norman and James Levine at Carnegie Hall (also in the

1990s). Her work has done much to lift the role of spirituals in modern life. This spiritual is called "Plenty Good Room."

Plenty Good Room

Plenty good room, plenty good room,
Plenty good room in my Father's kingdom,
Plenty good room, plenty good room,
Just choose your seat and sit down.

I would not be a sinner,
I'll tell you the reason why,
'cause if my Lord should call on me,
I wouldn't be ready to die.

Plenty good room...

I would not be a liar,
I'll tell you the reason why,
'cause if my Lord should call on me,
I wouldn't be ready to die.

Plenty good room...

I wouldn't be a backslider,
I'll tell you the reason why,
'cause if my Lord should call on me,
I wouldn't be ready to die.

Plenty good room...

(Available online. Suggested performer: Kathleen Battle)

William L. Dawson (1899–1990) was an African American composer, choir director, and professor born in 1899. His father had been a slave and was an illiterate day laborer. Dawson ran away from home when he was thirteen and enrolled in the precollege program at Tuskegee Institute under the tutelage of Booker T. Washington. He spent the next several years studying at different schools, ultimately chairing the music department at Tuskegee University. He was a gifted composer of both orchestral and choral music. A spiritual that he arranged was "Soon Ah Will Be Done."

Soon Ah Will Be Done

Soon Ah will be done-a with the troubles of the world
The troubles of the world
The troubles of the world
Soon Ah will be done-a with the troubles of the world
Goin' home to live with God.

I want, I want to meet my mother
I want, I want to meet my mother
I want, I want to meet my mother
I'm goin' to live with God

Soon Ah will be done-a with the troubles of the world
With the troubles of the world
With the troubles of the world
Soon Ah will be done with the troubles of the world)
Goin' home to live with God

No more, No more weepin' and a wailin'
No more, no more weepin' and a wailin'
No more, no more weepin' and a wailin'
I'm goin' to live with God

No more weepin' and a wailin'
No more weepin' and a wailin'
No more weepin' and a wailing
No more weepin' and a wailin'

No more weepin' and a wailin'
No more weepin
'No more weepin'

Soon Ah will be done-a with the troubles of this world
With the troubles of the world)
With the troubles of this world
Soon Ah will be done-a with the troubles of the world
Goin' home to live with God.

I want, I want to meet my Jesus
I want, I want to meet my Jesus
I want, I want to meet my Jesus
Goin' home to live with God

Soon Ah will be done-a with the troubles of the world
With the troubles of the world
With the troubles of the world
Soon Ah will be done-a with the troubles of the world
Goin' home to live with God.

No more, No more weepin' and a wailin'
No more, No more weepin' and a wailin',
No more weepin'. No more wailin'
Weepin' and a wailing, weepin' and a wailin'
Weepin' and a wailin'
I'm goin' home, goin' home to live with God

(Available online. Suggested performer: Atlanta Master
Chorale)

Finally, *William Francis Allen* (1830–1899), *Charles Pickard
Ware* (1840–1921), and *Lucy McKim Garrison* (1842–1877) were
monumental in the popularization of African American spirituals.
In 1867, they published the first-ever collection of these important
songs. They listened to the slaves in person and took down the musi-

cal notes as best they could. Sometimes, when possible, they listened to them several times. When they heard a different version, they put that down too. The person who began this effort was Lucy McKim Garrison. She arranged two of them, one of which was very popular in its time. It was called "Poor Rosy."

Poor Rosy

Poor Rosy, poor gal; Poor Rosy, poor gal;
Rosy break my poor heart, Heav'n shall-a be my home.
Poor Rosy, poor gal, Poor Rosy poor gal
Rosy break my poor heart, Heav'n shall-a be my home.

I cannot stay in hell one day, Heav'n shall-a be my home;
I sing and pray my soul away; Heav'n shall be my home.

O when I walk, I walk with God, Heav'n shall be my
*   home.*
O when I talk, I talk with God, Heav'n shall be my home.

Poor Rosy, poor gal; Poor Rosy, poor gal;
Rosy break my poor heart, Heav'n shall-a be my home.

(Available online. Suggested performer: William Appling Singers)

These artists represent just a few of the many influencers in the use of spirituals as a concert and popular repertoire. They include writers, singers, composers, and arrangers. Spirituals would not have achieved prominence in the mainstream without them.

---

[1] John Lovell Jr., *Black Song* (New York: The Macmillan Company, 1972), p. 452.

Harriet Tubman

From the very founding of our nation, slaveholders had to deal with the thorny issue of fugitive slaves. On May 12, 1786, "George Washington complained about a slave of his who escaped to Philadelphia toward 'a society of Quakers in the city formed for such purposes'. Not only were they fleeing, but they also found accomplices to assist them in crossing to freedom."[1] Harriet Tubman was such a freedom seeker.

Scholars debate how the term *underground railroad* emerged. By the 1840s, people were referring to the web of conspirators by that name. Georg Sheets of York, Pennsylvania, has claimed in his book *To the Setting of the Sun* that slaveowners looking for their "property" in York came up with the term. It is possible that this is true, as there was a factory there that built train cars, and the Baltimore and Ohio Railroad was connected to York. There was even an ex-slave in York, William C. Goodridge, who built railroad cars and sometimes used them to ferry escaping slaves to Philadelphia and parts of the north.

There is another version of the history of the term *underground railroad* according to Catherine Clinton in her biography of Harriet Tubman. In the year 1831, a slave named Tice Davids escaped his Kentucky home for freedom in Ohio. Seeing his owner hot on his trail, he jumped into the Ohio River and headed for the other shore. The owner slowed down because he had to search for a boat and said to someone on shore that the slave disappeared so quickly that he must have escaped on an underground road, hence the name Underground Railroad.

Harriet Tubman, alone and by herself, took the Philadelphia route of the Underground Railroad in September of 1849. She found it relatively uncomplicated to traverse, though it certainly was not an easy trip. She left a quilt with her first contact and got directions from each of her other contacts as she progressed. It is not known whether the quilt was a gift or a bribe, but she didn't have any serious problems after that. She got a ride at her first stop and proceeded the rest of the way on foot.

African Americans traveling by themselves had to have a pass with their owner's signature. The paper had to state that there was permission to be about the owner's business and what time or date they were due to return. This was one of the reasons owners wanted their slaves to be illiterate. The escaping slaves could all too easily forge passes otherwise. Because of this, escaping slaves had to travel at night and hide during the day. They also had to stay in rural areas where cover was more abundant.

A year after her escape to freedom, Tubman went south again to help some of her family escape. Since it proved to be a safe journey, she returned south many times to take others. She traveled as far north as St. Catherines, Canada, with escaping slaves and lived there for a while.

> She crafted her expeditions with extreme care. White abolitionist Alice Stone Blackwell reported that Moses [Tubman] would use gospel music and spirituals to signal to fugitives hidden along the road: "She directed them by her songs, as to whether they might show themselves, or must continue to lie low."[2]

One of those songs is "Swing Low, Sweet Chariot." Perhaps her favorite, it suggested to enslaved persons wanting to escape that she was in the area. "Home" was a symbol for Canada or, in the early days, before the Fugitive Slave Act of 1850, Philadelphia, a favorite city among escapees. Philadelphia had a large free black and fugitive slave population, and it was home to many Quakers and abolitionists. "Chariot" is said to be a code mention of the Underground Railroad.

Swing Low, Sweet Chariot

Oh, swing low, sweet chariot
Comin' for to carry me home.
Swing low, sweet chariot
Comin' for to carry me home.

I looked over Jordan and what did I see?
Comin' for to carry me home.
A band of angels comin' after me.
Comin' for to carry me home.

Oh, swing low, sweet chariot…

If you get there before I do,
Comin' for to carry me home.
Tell all my friends I'm a-comin' too.
Comin' for to carry me home.

Oh, swing low sweet chariot…

I'm sometimes up and sometimes down.
Comin' for to carry me home.
But still my soul feels heavenly bound.
Comin' for to carry me home.

Oh, swing low sweet chariot…

(Available online. Suggested performer: Paul Robeson)

Another famous spiritual associated with Harriet Tubman is "Go Down Moses." After many trips to the North, Harriet came to be known as the "Moses" of her people. The spiritual fit her mission completely. "Egypt's land" referred to the South, and "Let my people go" was a cry heard from every enslaved person. "Oppressed so hard they could not stand" surely fit the description of slavery in America, and as has been mentioned earlier, "Pharaoh" referred to the slaveowner or overseer.

Go Down Moses

When Israel was in Egypt's land, let my people go;
Oppressed so hard they could not stand, let my people go!

Go Down (go down), Moses (Moses), way down in Egypt's
   land;
Tell old Pharaoh to let my people go!

"Thus, saith the Lord" bold Moses said, "Let my people go!
If not, I'll smite your firstborn dead. Let my people go!"

Go down (go down), Moses (Moses), way down…

"No more in bondage shall they toil, Let my people go!
Let them come out with Egypt's spoil, let my people go!"

Go down (go down), Moses (Moses), way down…

(Available online. Suggested performer: Louis Armstrong)

Throughout the 1850s, Tubman became familiar with many stations on the Underground Railroad. They used the usual hiding places: potato cellars, attics, and barns. Some station masters constructed hidden rooms, secret tunnels, and fake closets.[3]

Frederick Douglass may have hosted a band that Harriet Tubman led. It is said that a group of eleven slaves stayed at his home in Rochester, New York, at a time when Tubman was known to be in the area. Most groups were not that large, but Tubman was fearless and was known for having taken on large groups of people.

During the Civil War, Harriet served in the Union army as a nurse, a scout, and a spy. She even led a force of black soldiers to rescue eight hundred slaves. She was the first woman, and certainly, the first black woman, to lead such an attack. She was called by some "General Tubman." After the war, she sheltered indigent African Americans at her home in Auburn, New York.

Harriet Tubman was a heroic person who used music to lead her people out of bondage. Spirituals offered a vehicle for sending messages to the persons who were in her care and for providing confidence among her passengers that she would not lead them astray.

---

[1] Catherine Clinton, *Harriet Tubman* (New York: Back Bay Books, Little Brown and Company, 2005), p. 39.

[2] Clinton, *Harriet Tubman*, p. 89.

[3] Clinton, *Harriet Tubman*, p. 70.

Frederick Douglass

Many people, both black and white, strongly promoted the abolition of slavery. Certainly, Harriet Tubman was one; another was Frederick Douglass.

Like Tubman, Douglass grew up on a plantation in Maryland. His childhood circumstances were more pleasant than hers. He spent his youth under the care of his grandmother with several other of his cousins. As a youngster, he was moved to servitude in the household of the "old master" where life became difficult. From there, he went to the household of the master's daughter in Baltimore. In her home, he was treated as if he were a member of the family and was even taught the alphabet. When the son of the family grew up, however, and Douglass got older, things became unbearable. This was when Douglass began dreaming of freedom and how he might escape slavery.

In his autobiography, *My Bondage and My Freedom*, Douglass made some comments about the place of music on a plantation.

> Slaves are generally expected to sing as well as work.
> A silent slave is not liked by masters or overseers.
> "Make a noise," "make a noise," and "bear a hand"
> are the words usually addressed to the slaves when
> there is silence amongst them. This may account

for the almost constant singing heard in the southern states. There was generally, singing among the teamsters, as it was one means of letting the overseers know where they were, and that they were moving on with the work.[1]

He described spirituals thusly:

They told a tale…loud, long, and deep, breathing the prayer and complaint of souls boiling over with the bitterest anguish. Every tone was a testimony against slavery and a prayer to God for deliverance from chains.[2]

"Keep A-inchin' Along" could be one of those songs.

Keep A-inchin' Along

Keep a-inchin' along,
Keep a-inchin' along,
Jesus will come by-and-by.
Keep a-inchin' along, like a poor inchworm,
Jesus will come by-and-by.

It was inch by inch that I sought the Lord,
Jesus will come by-and-by.
And inch by inch that he saved my soul,
Jesus will come by-and-by.

Keep a-inchin' along, Keep…

We'll inch and inch and inch along
Jesus will come by-and-by.
And inch and inch till we get home.
Jesus will come by-and-by.

Keep a-inchin' along, Keep…

(Available online. Suggested performer: Howard Gospel Choir)

Douglass tried to escape twice; the first attempt was made in a group. As they prepared to leave, they became more and more excited. They often sang the spiritual "I Am Bound for the Land of Canaan," which had a double or coded meaning for them.

> A keen observer might have detected in our repeated singing of "O Canaan, Sweet Canaan, I Am Bound for the Land of Canaan" something more than a hope of reaching heaven. We meant to reach the north— and the north was our Canaan.[3]

O Canaan, Sweet Canaan, I Am Bound for the Land
    of Canaan

O who will come and go with me?
I am bound for the land of Canaan.
Sweet Canaan's land I'm bound to see,
I am bound for the land of Canaan.
I'll join with them who've gone before
I'm bound for the land of Canaan.
Where sin and sorrow are no more,
I'm bound for the land of Canaan.

Oh, Canaan, bright Canaan,
I'm bound for the land of Canaan.
Oh, Canaan is my happy home,
I'm bound for the land of Canaan.

(Available online as "Sweet Canaan." Suggested performer: Deborah Anne Goss)

Douglass wasn't successful in this first endeavor. Someone from their group reported them to the authorities. Fortunately, the runaways escaped a trip to the auction block as there was no proof, and Douglass's owner didn't really believe that Frederick would want to take flight. However, they were watched more carefully.

Douglass wasn't treated especially poorly by this owner, but he had had it with slavery and watched for another opportunity to run. This time, he planned to escape by himself.

After the first attempt, Douglass was sent back to Baltimore, Maryland, where he had lived a good life. It was no longer good. His owner treated him much more cruelly than he had in the past. After some deliberation between them, Douglass persuaded the owner to let him find his own work on the docks. The owner drove a hard bargain but eventually relented. Over time, Frederick was able to acquire enough money to disguise himself as a sailor and gain passage on a boat sailing to Philadelphia, Pennsylvania. Not feeling safe in Philadelphia, he traveled on to New York City and then to New Bedford, Massachusetts. New Bedford was a haven for escaped slaves. He was welcomed, and he gloried in his freedom.

Soon after he reached New Bedford, Douglass came across a publication, *The Liberator*, edited by William Lloyd Garrison, the famous abolitionist. He studied it carefully and found that its activist message was one with which he fully agreed. Not long after that, Douglass began speaking at abolitionist events and made a great impact. He did that for fourteen years and finally wrote the first edition of his autobiography about life as a slave.

This first publication endangered him as a free man. He decided to go to England, where he eventually met Queen Victoria. He ultimately returned to America, where he felt he could be of better service in the cause of freedom.

Douglass moved to Rochester, New York, where he published an abolitionist paper called *The North Star* and continued to enjoy success as a lecturer. He did not receive much encouragement from his American friends. They feared for him. They thought it was not good to announce that he was an escaped slave to the public. They were certain that there would be new attempts to capture him.

Nonetheless, his English friends pushed him to go forward with the idea. And he did. He received help from people such as the abolitionist Harriet Jacobs, who moved to Rochester with her grown son, to help him with his publication of *The North Star.*

He closed his autobiography with the following:

> Believing that one of the best means of emancipating the slaves of the south is to improve and elevate the character of the free colored people of the north I shall labor in the future, as I have labored in the past, to promote the moral, social, religious, and intellectual elevation of the free colored people; never forgetting my own humble origin, nor refusing, while heaven lends me ability, to use my voice, my pen, or my vote, to advocate the great and primary work of the universal and unconditional emancipation of my entire race.[4]

---

[1] *My Freedom and My Bondage* (Odin's Library Classics), p. 33.
[2] *My Freedom and My Bondage*, p. 33.
[3] *My Freedom and My Bondage*, p. 98.
[4] *My Freedom and My Bondage*, p. 144.

CHAPTER 20

Summary

Slaves from western and central Africa arrived on American soil early in the sixteenth and seventeenth centuries. They brought their tradition of song, dance, and religion with them. These would evolve into an art form known as the spiritual.

In the South, it was illegal for slaves to read and write, so Negroes turned to song and dance as a means of communication. They sang songs that had secret meanings, known only to them, and they shared them by rote. Later, as the slaves became acquainted with American religion, Old Testament Bible stories became a big part of their songs. Ring shouts, such as "Oh, Eve, Where Is Adam?" were the earliest examples of spirituals. They exist along the South Carolina and Georgia coasts to this day.

Since the latter half of the nineteenth century, oral tradition has provided us with information about secret codes, symbols, and masking. Stories of code-bearing songs persist still and are associated with the Underground Railroad. Spirituals such as "Swing Low, Sweet Chariot" called a slave to join a conductor on the "chariot" to freedom. Songs such as "Follow the Drinking Gourd" described a map out of bondage. Spirituals that referred to Canaan were allusions to the North and Canada.

Spirituals took many forms. Sorrow songs, jubilee songs, and work songs were common. The sorrow song, "Sometimes I Feel Like a Motherless Child," tells the poignant story of a child on the auction block. "This Little Light of Mine" is a jubilee song, one of joy, as its name implies. It is accompanied by hand clapping and perhaps foot stomping. "Jump Down, Turn Around" is a work song for picking cotton. The tempo of the song helps set the pace for the work effort. Often, these songs contain syncopation and/or call and response.

As slaves spread across the Americas, spirituals took on new forms. For instance, in the Bahamas, the "rhyming spiritual" developed with sponge fishermen. Many sea shanties had their origins in the Bahamas. They were seldom religious and usually work songs but sung by African men (both slave and free) on sailing ships headed all over the world: Australia, Massachusetts, Florida, San Francisco, Mexico, Canada, and many other ports of call. The whole of the seventeenth century through the early twentieth century involved sailing ships with African American crews.

Abolitionists played a big role in the Underground Railroad. They were conductors and stationmasters. They were in small towns such as Elmira, New York, and in big cities such as Philadelphia, Pennsylvania. Some helped thousands escape, and others helped just a few. Some abolitionists were white, others black. Some were violent, others peaceful. Women and men both took on the cause, and groups as well as individuals had a great impact.

Mexico and Florida played major roles in the Underground Railroad, Florida, as a haven for a while and later as an escape route to the Bahamas. The Black Seminoles brought their music from Florida to Mexico.

Escaped slaves like Harriet Tubman and Frederick Douglass were strongly influenced by African American spirituals. Both were born on plantations in Maryland and found their own way to freedom. They each became active abolitionists after their escapes. "Go Down Moses" is a spiritual that was used as a calling card for Tubman, dubbed "the Moses of her people." Douglass sang "Oh Canaan, Sweet Canaan" as he prepared for attempted escapes.

A great many people helped move spirituals into the mainstream. The Fisk University Jubilee Singers were among the first to take on the task. Artists such as Marian Anderson and Paul Robeson played a role. More recent singers such as Kathleen Battle have done much to elevate the awareness of this type of African American music. "He's Got the Whole World in His Hands," "No More Auction Block for Me," and "Plenty Good Room" are representative spirituals of these artists.

Religion was a difficult issue in the minds of slaves and slaveholders alike. At first, slaves didn't want anything to do with Christianity. They were happy with their religious practices from Africa, but slaveowners didn't like the practice of religion of any sort by their slaves. They felt that their African religion was heathen and that slaves identified too closely with Jesus and the Hebrews who escaped bondage with the help of the Christian God. They didn't want their slaves to get any ideas. Ultimately, Christianity was adopted by most slaves, and slaveowners tolerated their passion for it.

The evolution of the spiritual saw its beginnings in unadulterated African songs, taken almost in whole from Africa. It claimed American heritage as well by calling on the name of the God of the Old Testament and Jesus Christ of the New Testament. Styles of spirituals, which developed earlier in slavery, remained an important part of its tradition and continued as jazz, blues, and gospel up to the present day.

The genre of the African American spiritual plays an unparalleled part in the history of music. It transports us back in time and propels us forward into a better understanding of African American heritage and culture. This last spiritual, "Over My Head, I Hear Music in the Air," speaks for generations, past and present, of African Americans and their fight against oppression.

Over My Head, I Hear Music in the Air

Over my head, I hear music in the air.
Over my head, I hear music in the air.
Over my head, I hear music in the air,
There must be a God somewhere.

(Available online. Suggested performer: Kathleen Battle)

ACKNOWLEDGMENTS

The museums I would like to acknowledge are the Library of Congress; the Smithsonian National Museum of African American History and Culture in Washington, DC; the Musical Instrument Museum, Phoenix, Arizona; the Harriet Tubman Museum and Educational Center, Cambridge, Maryland; the Harriet Tubman Home, Auburn, New York; the John W. Jones Museum in Elmira, New York; the Starr Clark Tin Shop in Mexico, New York; New-York Historical Society; and Chemung County New York Historical Society.

As with any project of this kind, many contribute to the finished product. I especially want to acknowledge the help of my sister Susan Ameigh, who accompanied me on several research trips and read the manuscript for editing purposes many times before I sent it to the publisher. She also contributed the drawing for the cover. I would like to acknowledge the help of my brother Dr. Michael S. Ameigh, PhD, who read it several times also and suggested some structural changes, which I appreciated. I want to thank Dr. Wayne Wold, DMA, who is a mentor of mine and gave me the suggestion to write this book as well as read it for me. I am grateful to Dr. Melanie Zeck, librarian, at the American Folklife Center, Library of Congress, who helped me research the Bahamas music connection as well as the Mexican connection. I appreciate the help of Sibyl Mose, who accompanied me on two research trips and read the manuscript for editing purposes. Judy, my friend Judith Kehoe contributed as well. I especially thank her for introducing me to a documentary on Seminole music. James Hotchkiss and Allie Proud were kind enough to guide me through the Starr Clark Tin Shop, Mexico, New York, and answer several questions about the Underground Railroad in their part of the country. I want to thank Cleveland Thrower at the John W. Jones Museum for his help with the research in Elmira, New York. Also, I would like to thank "Willie" for the use of his likeness on the cover.

I would also like to recognize Robert Rozelle, deceased, my high school music teacher who introduced me to my favorite spiritual, "Soon Ah Will Be Done" Arr. by William Dawson. I would also like to recognize my fifth graders at Walkersville Middle School, who got me started on this adventure. (They are all adults now.) I would like to acknowledge my class at Frederick Community College, who taught me much.

Included Spirituals

Selected Recordings

Anderson, Marian. "Marian Anderson: He's Got the Whole World in His Hands." New York: BMG Music Classics (originally RCA Victor), 1994.

Anderson, Marian. *Marian Anderson*. New York: RCA Victor, 1989.

Battle, Kathleen, and Jessye Norman. *Spirituals in Concert*. Hamburg, Germany: Deutsche Grammophon, 1991.

Franklin, Aretha. *Amazing Grace*. New York: Atlantic Recording Company, 1972. Released.

Hayes, Roland. *Favorite Spirituals*. New York: Vanguard Classics, 1995.

Jackson, Mahalia. *Best Loved Spirituals*. New York: Sony, 1993.

Jackson, Mahalia. *Gospels, Spirituals and Hymns*. New York: Columbia Records, 1991.

Johnson Reagon, Bernice, compiler. *Wade in the Water, Vol. I: African American Spirituals: The Concert Tradition*. Washington, DC.: Smithsonian Institution/Folkways Recordings, 1994.

Johnson Reagon, Bernice, compiler. *Wade in the Water, Vol. II: African American Congregational Singing*. Washington, DC: Smithsonian Institution/Folkways Recordings 1994.

McIntosh County Shouters. *The McIntosh County Shouters: Slave Shout Songs from the Coast of Georgia*. Washington, DC: Smithsonian/Folkways Recordings, 1984.

Norman, Jessye, with the Ambrosian Singers and Willis Patterson, conductor. *Spirituals.* Phillips, 1978.

Odetta. *Christmas Spirituals.* Waterbury, VT: Alcazar Productions, 1988.

Price, Leontyne. *Leontyne Price Sings Spirituals.* RCA Legacy (manufactured on demand by Amazon).

Ragin, Derek Lee, with Moses Hogan and the New World Ensemble. *Ev'ry Time I Feel the Spirit: Spirituals.* Englewood, NJ: Channel Classics, 1991.

Robeson, Paul. *The Power and the Glory.* New York: Columbia Records, 1991.

BIBLIOGRAPHY

"Invisible History, Middle Florida's Hidden Roots. PBS video.

"La Bamba: The Afro-Mexican Story." Afro Pop Worldwide. March 3, 2022.

Allen, William Francis, et al. *Slave Songs of the United Slaves*. Pantianos Classics.

Baumgartner, Alice L. *South to Freedom: Runaway Slaves to Mexico and the Road to the Civil War*. Basic Books, 2020.

Bebey, Francis. *African Music: A People's Art*. Reprinted in translation. Lawrence Hill Books, 1975.

Berlin, Ira, Marc Favreau, and Steven F. Miller (eds.). *Remembering Slavery: African Americans Talk about Their Personal Experiences of Slavery and Emancipation*. New York: The New Press, 1996.

Bolster, Jeffrey. *Black Jacks, African American Seamen in the Age of Sail*. Harvard University Press, 1998.

Buis, Johann S. (Musical Transcriptions and Historical Essay). *Shout Because You're Free: The African American Ring Shout Tradition in Coastal Georgia*. Athens and London: The University of Georgia Press, 1998.

Burnett, John. *NPR: All Things Considered: A Chapter in US History Often Ignored: The Flight of Runaway Slaves to Mexico*. February 28, 2021.

Clinton, Catherine. *Harriet Tubman: The Road to Freedom*. (Back Bay Books/Little Brown and Company, 2005.

Douglass, Frederick. *My Bondage and My Freedom*. Odin's Library Classics, 2022.

Du Bois, W. E. B. *The Souls of Black Folk.* Millennium Publications, 2014.

Edwards, Charles Lincoln. *Bahama Songs and Stories.* Forgotten Books, 2015.

Grant, Richard. "South to the Promised Land." *Smithsonian* Vol. 53/03.

Guenther, Eileen. *In Their Own Words, Slave Life and the Power of Spirituals.* MorningStar Music Publishers, 2016.

Jacobs, Harriet. *Incidents in the Life of a Slave Girl, Seven Years Concealed.*

Johnson, James Weldon, and J. Rosamond Johnson. *American Negro Spirituals, Two Volumes in One.* New York: Viking Press, 1969.

Jones, Arthur C. *Wade in the Water: The Wisdom of the Spirituals.* Boulder, CO: Leave a Little Room, 2005.

Lovell, John Jr. *Black Song: The Forge and the Flame.* New York: The Macmillan Company, 1972.

Martin, Michel. *NPR, Tell Me More: Listen to a Holler: Songs of Slavery.* January 2, 2008.

Miller, Terry, and Andrew Shahriari. Third edition, Chapter 11. In *World Music: A Global Journey.* Routledge, 2012.

Palmer, Colin A. *Slaves of the White God: Blacks in Mexico 1570–1650.* Harvard University Press, 1976.

Parrish, Lydia. *Slave Songs of the Georgia Sea Islands.* Athens and London: The University of Georgia Press, 1992.

Raboteau, Albert J. *Slave Religion: The "Invisible Institution" in the Antebellum South.* Oxford, New York; Toronto, Melbourne: Oxford University Press, 1980.

Rosenbaum, Art (Text and Drawings) Rosenbaum, Margo Newmark (Photographs). *Shout Because You're Free, the African American Ring Shout Tradition in Coastal Georgia.* Athens and London: The University of Georgia, 2013.

Sheets, Georg R. *To the Setting of the Sun: The Story of York.* Windsor Publications, 1981.

Still, William. *The Underground Railroad: Authentic Narratives and First-Hand Accounts.* Edited by Ian Frederick Finseth. Dover Publications Inc., 2007.

Talley, Patricia Ann, editor and representative in Mexico for the Dr. Martin Luther King Jr. Task Force in Southfield, Michigan. *Imagine-Mexico.com/Soul Music from the Black Seminoles of Mexico.* January 2022.

ABOUT THE AUTHOR

An educator, conductor, organist, and composer, author Truuke M. Ameigh has had a lifelong interest in spirituals. Beginning with school as a youth, spirituals were a source of inspiration. She has taught them and about them as a church musician, a conductor, a public-school music teacher, and a professor. She wrote and published a children's book about spirituals called *Gonna Sing!* and has had several organ arrangements published, including an arrangement of *Wade in the Water.* As a church musician, she has been a recitalist in many venues, and her career as a teacher and as a church musician has offered innumerable opportunities to conduct this remarkable literature.